Beyond Amuck

Beyond Amuck

More Hobby Farm Adventures

Sue Stein

2017
Dragonstone Press
Rosemount, Minnesota

Beyond Amuck
Copyright © 2017 by Sue Stein

First Edition August 2017

All rights reserved.
Printed in the United States of America

No part of this book may be used or reproduced in any manner whatsoever without written permission from the publisher except in the case of brief quotations embodied in critical articles and reviews.

ISBN: 978-0-9991801-0-5
Library of Congress Control Number: 2017911582

Cover photo © Nataliya Hora/Shutterstock.com
All other photos © Sue Stein

Dragonstone Press
3820 120th St. W.
Rosemount, Minnesota 55068
www.dragonstonepress.com

Also by the author:
Amuck: Tales From a Hobby Farm
Haiku for the Soul

Website: SueSteinAuthor.com
Contact the author: stei0010@gmail.com

To Bridget, who was there for the "fun"

Contents

1	Weird and Wonderful	1
2	Feed Store Follies	11
3	A Smashing Good Time	15
4	Alpaca Angst	25
5	Horsing Around	29
6	Board Silly	33
7	Getting Buzzed	41
8	Feathered Fiends	45
9	The Dark Side	53
10	What the Hay?	61
11	Another Baaaad Idea	67
12	Boundaries: What Are Those?	77
13	Swim With the Fishes	87
14	Bird Brains	91
15	Running With the Rodents	97
16	Swan Lake	101
17	A Plague of Coyotes	105
18	Day Tripping	113
19	A Wheelie Good Thing	121
20	A Horse is a Horse, Of Course, Of Course…	127
21	Dog Days	129
22	Simply Nuts	135
23	Chicken-Hearted	143
24	Flown the Coop	151
25	The Bobcat Returns	159
26	Feathers Flew	161
27	Going Batty	173

28	Nine Lives	177
29	It's Time to Go	183
30	Heaven is a Hammock	189
31	The Cone of Shame	193
32	Revenge is Sweet	197
33	Fun and Games	199

1

Weird and Wonderful

Sitting on the front steps one afternoon with my dog Breezy, I heard an odd bird-type of sound, and it seemed to be coming closer. I looked up from the book I was reading to witness two bald eagles streaking along only ten feet above the ground, winging right at us. They noticed us about the same time and adjusted their trajectory slightly to fly between the garage and the side of the house. As they blasted past, neck and neck with each other, they glanced nonchalantly to their right at my dog Breezy and me. Their eyes met mine and I'm fairly certain my mouth was hanging fully agape. They were so close—and so huge. Their attention was quickly drawn to the chicken coop to their left and their heads swung in unison to view a possible snack. Alas, they were going far too fast and they arrowed off like intercontinental ballistic missiles to my backyard. All of this happened in mere seconds and I was still attempting to process the whole thing when they reappeared after circumnavigating my house, and were soon engaged in making lazy circles above one of the ponds. *What in the heck was that all about?* I wondered. Were they fighting? Engaged in mating behavior? Just working off their lunch? I struggled to remember bald eagle breeding times in Minnesota and thought eagles mate and lay their eggs by February, and it was now late May. Maybe these two were late starters. Who knows? It's not like as they flew past they croaked, "We're just popping by to say hi." Although that may have been what the weird bird noises meant. I'll have to brush up on my Eagle Speak for our next encounter.

It seems nearly every time I sit out on those steps, *something* happens. Some type of wild critter hops, flies, trots, or slithers past. What am I talking about—it isn't only the front steps, it's everywhere in the yard surrounding my house. Not a day goes by when I'm working on my computer at the dining room table and movement in the backyard catches my eye. *What now?* I usually mutter in irritation as I once again stop what I was doing and look up to catch sight of another animal travelling past the back of my house. I swear my yard is the equivalent of an animal superhighway. Instead of an autobahn, my yard is an animalbahn, filled with urkeys, geese, ducks, eagles, hawks, huge pileated woodpeckers, coyotes, deer, woodchucks, and bunnies. Lots of bunnies. You know what they say about bunnies—they breed like bunnies. Enough said.

You name it, I've pretty much seen it sauntering past at any hour

Wild turkeys parading past my back window
on their way to who knows where

of the day or night, or stopping and hanging out, watching me while I'm watching it. High noon and a lone coyote trots past as I look out my window? Ha! That's nothing new in my neck of the woods as the coyotes don't seem to care what time it is. They need a refresher in coyote etiquette: sleep all day and hunt all night. Perhaps I'll remind the next one I see. Well, then again, maybe not. They aren't the cuddliest of creatures. I've had enough run ins with them in the past to know I don't want to interact more closely than I've already been forced to do to protect my dogs and livestock, not to mention myself.

The many coyote incidents in particular have caused me untold amounts of stress and contributed to my logarithmically increasing grey hair count. Oftentimes when I'm outside, I feel the need to be hypervigilant and always watch my back, scanning for any sign of danger, ready to defend myself and my animals. Which sucks, when you think about it. It's hard to enjoy my land if I'm worrying what might be about to happen when I step out the door holding an ancient wooden baseball bat as defense.

Periodically, things simmer down and I relax my guard and blithely go about my business outside with nary a care in the world. And then it happens again. The coyotes become too comfortable and think they own the place. The baseball bat gets hauled out and dusted off, my guard goes back up, and I'm forced to take the following steps when I let the dogs outside: Hold the door open. Look in all directions before I take a step out the door, day or night. Continuously scan the surrounding woods and pasture for any movement. Watch Breezy to see if she is alerting on something and follow her gaze to discern any hidden predators while keeping her from bolting off after them.

It's rather exhausting to always be on guard. People may think I'm nuts but, although I live in the frozen tundra otherwise known as Minnesota, I prefer winter over summer, because the animal tracks are visible in the snow. I can see what has been in the yard the night before, and where it has travelled. Tracks come in from all directions from the woods and pasture and traverse my backyard. A fresh snowfall is soon covered by the beaten-down trails of animals of every kind making their way from one place to another.

Sometimes I'm astounded by the sheer number of different kinds of wildlife—I see the tracks of deer, coyotes, some huge paws which may or may not be a local bobcat, bunnies, raccoons, opossums, mice, and squirrels. A multitude of deer tracks this last winter covered my front steps as they made their way to the bird feeder to empty it out in the dark of night.

How did I get here—meaning, how did I find myself the owner of a hobby farm populated by various farm animals, and dealing with numerous animal-related catastrophes and utter mayhem? Well, that's easy. I moved back to the property where I was raised, which I inherited when my parents passed away. Growing up here as a child, I spent nearly every waking moment out in the pasture or the woods, exploring. Nature and animals are my first love, and as a child I dreamed of someday having my own horse. I'm not sure how that eventually translated as an adult into two miniature horses, hordes of chickens, a llama, three alpacas, and most recently, a goat. How that happened, I'm not entirely certain, particularly as I'm doing this completely on my own. When people, particularly women, learn that I'm taking care of nearly twenty acres and assorted farm animals with no help, they invariably look at me, eyes wide with horror, and say, "You do that all *yourself?*" I'm not sure whether they think it's a good thing or unbelievably horrifying, as they usually quickly change the subject. Even I can't decide. It all depends on the day and what new mayhem has occurred.

It's not only the livestock that makes my life so interesting; it's the wildlife as well. Pretty much every wild critter known to the state of Minnesota has appeared in my yard at one point; well, everything except a moose. Although I wouldn't hold my breath; weirder things have happened around here. The most frequent and unwelcome visitors, particularly when they show up in my yard in the middle of the afternoon, are the coyotes. I made the mistake of watching a documentary on public television one night about coy-wolves—a hybrid of coyote and timber wolf. I can't think of a more lethal combination—highly intelligent wolf mixed with cunning and sneaky coyote—and yes, I've seen them here. Regular coyotes typically are skinny and have a rust-red coat, a long, narrow snout, and crazy, feral eyes. The coy-wolves' coats are grey to black, their snouts and heads are wider and broader, and their bodies are larger and stockier than coyotes. They stare unflinchingly into your eyes, the intelligence in their gaze so at odds with that of the regular coyotes I've faced. And I've faced too many of both of these animals for my taste over the years since I moved back. They consider my yard their territory, and my dogs as interlopers to be killed. Unfortunately, I've had to run into the fray to save my dogs a number of times, and I'm thankful that so far the coyotes have eventually left each time without attacking me.

One day a woodchuck stopped by to say hi while I was taking a well-deserved nap in the porch. I heard a scratching at the screen door and I opened my eyes to see it standing outside the door, smiling at me. It certainly looked like a smile. Then one of my dogs, who had been sleeping next to me, saw it and went nuts, barking and running towards the door. I watched as the woodchuck slowly wandered across the lawn and disappeared into the rose bushes by the chicken coop. Later that day when I went to feed the mini horses it popped up out of the weeds like a jack-in-the-box, seeming to say, *Hey! Here I am again!* I hadn't freaked out when it tried to get into the porch, but this was like a scene from a horror movie and I couldn't help it; I screamed and ran. It was truly strange.

Among the hordes of raccoons populating my property, one raccoon in particular had a habit of showing up at 9PM on the dot every night one winter, climbing the cedar siding on the back of my house with his sharp claws to snack from the bird feeder hanging close to the bay window. I placed the feeder there to give the cats a vicarious thrill as they sat in the house watching birds flitting in for a bite to eat. So close, and yet so far.

Exactly at 9PM, like clockwork, that raccoon arrived. It made me wonder if he had a Raccoon Rolex. The sound of claws scrabbling on wood could be heard as he worked his way up the side of the house to attain optimal height opposite the feeder. All he then had to do was reach way, way out with one paw while holding tightly onto the siding with the other appendages, grab the bird feeder, swing it toward him, and dig in.

Nutter, one of my cats, liked to sit in the bay window and watch the raccoon. One night, hearing the raccoon making his ponderous way up the side of the house, I decided to stick my face right onto the glass nearest the raccoon, only a foot or two from his furry little face. He looked at me for a moment and went right back to chowing down on sunflower seeds and peanuts, ignoring me. Finally deciding there must be plenty of other things that damn raccoon could find to eat, I began taking down the bird feeder before dark each night.

Scrabbling claws commenced on time, and I snickered to myself, knowing the bird food buffet no longer existed for the hungry varmint. I snuck up to the window next to Nutter and peeked out. *Bwaahaahaa!* An evil laugh escaped my mouth. I had foiled him. He looked towards Nutter and me with a vaguely disappointed expression. There may have also been an audible sigh as he turned to shimmy back down to the ground. He returned several more nights until finally realizing the buffet was permanently closed, and vamoosed in the future to points unknown.

Critter sightings here seem to increase in the spring, as mating season for the various species goes into full swing. Gazing down at the mass of sprouting weeds and wondering when I'd have time to tackle them, much less the inclination, I walked through the flower bed near the front step. As I went past the hostas, I had a creepy feeling. And no wonder because soon afterward, while I sat on the front steps, I watched as a large snapping turtle emerged from beneath the hostas and trundled off like a little bulldozer across the front lawn, leaving a trail of flattened grass in her wake. She must have been laying eggs under the hostas. My bare feet were inches from her jaws and I'm thankful she didn't bite down on me as I walked past where she was hidden.

Usually the snapping turtles lay eggs along the edge of the front lawn near the driveway. This past spring saw a bumper crop of snappers; they were everywhere laying their eggs. Two days in a row one crawled to lay her eggs on top of the pile of horse manure and straw near the mini horses' pen. I laughed when I saw her perched there and she looked at me with a cold reptilian gaze as if to say, *What are you laughing about?* I left her to her egg-laying and went to the chicken coop to feed the chickens only to nearly trip over another snapper laying her eggs in the chicken manure/straw mixture I had piled outside after cleaning the coop. Next morning, all the eggs had been dug up and the contents sucked out, probably by raccoons, although I wouldn't put it past the possums. All that was left were curled-up white eggshells. All that effort she expended in crawling step by slow step up the steep hill from the pond, over to the chicken coop, and then the energy of laying a passle of eggs, all for naught. Well, the raccoon was happy about it, I'm sure. Mama snapper would have been ticked if she knew.

I'd forgotten that the snapping turtle had laid eggs on the horse manure pile until many months later when I finally moved the pile. What can I say? Sometimes it takes me a while before I get around to doing such delightful chores. Can you blame me? As I dug down with the pitchfork, lifting and slinging the accumulated manure, I uncovered three separate areas of egg laying. I felt like a paleontologist uncovering fossilized dinosaur eggs. None of the turtle eggs had ever hatched, probably because the manure was too concentrated, leaving the eggs brown-stained. I pitch-forked massive quantities of them. It was rather revolting, to say the least.

Weird critter encounters don't happen only in my yard; they occur frequently out on the gravel road as well. I live near the end of a mile-and-a-half road, in an area that is still rural, though it's close to the ever-expanding suburbs. One area of the road in particular is a major thoroughfare for critters to cross—I've seen deer, turkeys, turtles, crayfish, muskrats, snakes, fuzzy brown and black caterpillars, even a salamander or two making their way across. Ducks and geese hang out on the edge of the road in the early summer with their extended families. One day as I drove down the road, a coyote was lying dead in the middle, hit by a car. After my history with coyotes, it's no wonder that I stopped my car, gazed down at its body, and sneered at it. *About time one of you got nailed,* I thought. My dogs were in the back seat and I knew they shared my sentiments.

The funniest thing I think I've witnessed was when I saw a lone crayfish crossing the road in late May. Somehow I noticed something small moving across the road and stopped my car to see what it was. Was it a baby turtle? Nope. It was a full-grown crayfish. I watched as it journeyed across the road from one pond to the other. Sticking my head out the window, I struck up a conversation with him, although he was a bit reticent. "What the heck are you doing?" I asked. He halted his forward progress and looked up at me, then kept going. Another day I saw a different crayfish crossing. Who knows, it could have been the same one. This time he raised his pincers above his head in a clear threat of violence as my car bore down upon him. It was so ridiculous looking that I cracked up laughing. Did it really think it could take on a 2,000 pound piece of metal and win? No, I didn't run it over. I've been known to save baby snapping turtles from certain death; I certainly wouldn't run over a crayfish. My niece has seen them too, and we both scratched our heads. Crayfish crossing the road. For what possible reason? Was one pond not enough for them? Perhaps they were heading to their vacation hideaway.

Turtles of all shapes and sizes regularly take their shells into their hands and brave the road. Seeing them, I slam on the brakes, hop out, and help them across. All except for the big snapping turtles. They don't want your help. They would rather bite you first. The cutest turtle encounter I've witnessed was when a full-size painted turtle and a baby turtle were making a break for it together. I've never seen that happen before. I didn't think turtles had maternal instincts. How could they, when they lay their clutch of eggs and leave the hatching to chance?

I might be more observant of wildlife than other people, or maybe the wildlife around here just likes to mess with me. I was busily jotting down a story on my computer about the dogs, only to look up from where I sat at my laptop at the dining room table to see a grey squirrel hanging onto the cedar siding and looking in the bay window at me. It locked eyes with me and practically stared a hole in me. I think it wants to make sure that I write a story about the squirrels, too. Not to worry, fuzzy guy, I will.

With how comfortable all the wildlife seem to be around here I wouldn't be surprised in the least if, one of these days, one of the damn things knocks on my door, lets itself into the house, hunkers down on the couch next to the dog to watch TV, and demands I bring it a cold one. Seriously, I can see it happening. Especially to me, with all of the weird things that seem to occur in my general vicinity.

2

FEED STORE FOLLIES

Another day, another trip to the local feed store. If it's not hungry mini horses, it's ravenous chickens. The next day finds me picking up cat or dog food. Later, I will realize that I forgot to pick up cat litter—not a good thing to run out of when you have several cats—and back to the feed store I go. One of the employees, seeing me walk in for the third time that week, said, "Are you back *already?*" To which I jokingly told her I was fairly certain I single-handedly funded the recent addition to their building. She thought for a second and said, "You know, you're probably right." I think she was kidding.

On this particular feed store run, when I drove my car over to load the hay bale I'd purchased, I noticed in front of me a brand-new Hyundai sedan, its owner putting hay in the trunk. You'd think a normal person would have a truck or something else to load hay into, rather than a shiny new car, but no…here was a regular-looking guy tossing a bale of messy alfalfa hay into his pristine trunk. I shamelessly do this myself at least twice a week, but I've never claimed to be "normal" in any way, shape, or form. Watching this guy got me to thinking about what regular people would think if they witnessed this. Wouldn't they think, "That's disgusting. What's *wrong* with that guy?"

Eventually it was my turn and I pulled my car forward, got out, and turned to the employee loading the hay in my trunk. "So…" I ventured, "It looks like I'm not the only lunatic who does this."

"Oh, no. Lots of people do," he said as he maneuvered the bale into my car's trunk, chunks of alfalfa dropping left and right.

"Whew. That's good to know." I hopped back in and drove off, feeling somewhat better about my chances of possibly fitting into normal society.

I do admit to being somewhat embarrassed whenever I need to open the trunk in front of someone, considering so much hay remains inside the trunk after each hay bale is removed. Good lord, if I ever run out of hay, I could feed my mini horses right out of the trunk. In fact, after unloading the bale one day I left the trunk open, only to later see the goat hop inside and start chowing down. Seeing Donald standing in the trunk cracked me up.

One day I had to open the trunk in front of a friend. Warning her that it wouldn't be pretty, I popped open the trunk. She glanced inside and exclaimed in horror, "Oh, gross! I can't believe you have that in there!" But she's a city slicker, so she would never see the need to load hay in a car trunk. I didn't have the heart to tell her that I've had to put bales in the back seat on occasion—that might have put her over the edge. I've been able to fit three bales in my car, not a minor feat, if I do say so myself. One went in the trunk, and two were stuffed in the back seat. I was rather proud of myself that time, as I had to really work to get that second bale atop the first on the back seat. To this day I don't know how I did it. Getting the bales out was entirely too much fun—that took ingenuity and brute-force strength.

Using blankets to cover the seats and floor prior to loading the bales on the seat only does so much to keep the mess at bay. To this day, tiny bits of hay are still stuck in the ceiling liner above the back seat. I smile whenever I see them. Luckily no one ever sits in the back seat of my car—the sharp bits would probably put an eye out.

Sitting in my car one day waiting at a stoplight behind a mini van, I noticed the stick people stickers plastered on the back window: Mom, Dad, two kids, two dogs, and six bunnies. I started thinking about what it would look like if I put stickers like that on the back window of my car. The thought amused me to no end and I burst out laughing, because I'm fairly certain the entire back window would be *covered* in stickers. I might also need to continue them on the side windows.

At the time, the livestock situation here included, let's see…two dogs, four cats, two mini horses, and twenty-three bantam chickens. My God, just imagine it—the chickens alone would have taken up the majority of the rear window. A few years prior, more stickers would have been needed when I also owned a llama and three alpacas. Hmmm…I wonder if they sell alpaca stickers? That would be even funnier—I can imagine the people in the cars behind mine scratching their heads, wondering what the heck kind of stick animal it was. My car would sport one stick woman, along with a veritable Noah's ark of stick animals covering all available window space. The drivers would have to pull up next to me and crane their necks to see what kind of a looney tune was driving the car.

3

A Smashing Good Time

Living on a hobby farm and taking care of animals means having to do things you don't really want to do, and really don't know how to do, like build chicken runs, pound in fence posts, string fencing, shovel copious quantities of delightfully fresh manure...you get the idea. Considering I tend to be clumsy and prone to injury at the best of times, it's no wonder I've managed to injure myself to varying degrees, on a number of occasions.

One day a number of years ago, I spent part of an afternoon tearing apart an old wood dog kennel, an eyesore that was beginning to bother even me. I'd put it off for far too long already. It was time to grab the sledgehammer and get to work. I started smashing the plywood panels apart and decided destroying things was kind of fun. *Smash! Bang!* Somehow I managed to avoid taking out my kneecaps as I swung the sledgehammer with abandon. That was a miracle in itself.

Tossing each nailed panel aside onto the grass as I wrenched it apart like the Incredible Hulk after smashing it free, I decided to take a well-deserved break, and turned to walk back to the house. Once again wearing my ubiquitous Crocs, I had barely taken two steps before I managed to place a foot firmly on one of the discarded panels. Shall I mention this panel had landed with nails upward after I tossed it onto the ground? As in, rusted nails dating back to the early 1960s?

Suffice it to say Crocs are no match for rusty nails. Not one, but *two* nails swiftly pierced the bottom of my trusty Crocs. And just as inevitably, swiftly pierced the bottom of my right foot. There I was, standing with a sledgehammer clutched in a death grip in my left hand, and impaled by nails in my right foot. It hurt like *hell*. Dropping the sledgehammer and gingerly raising my foot, I gritted my teeth, reached down and wrenched the wood panel free of my foot.

Holy crap. That was *not* pleasant.

Dropping onto the ground, I sat and removed the traitorous Croc, pulled the foot towards me, and marveled at the blood pouring from the two puncture wounds. I hobbled/hopped all the way back to the house, where I doused the holes with hydrogen peroxide and then bandaged them once they stopped bubbling. I hadn't had a tetanus shot in years, so my next step was to make a doctor appointment.

I hate to admit it, but I did the same damn thing several years later. And a few years after that. Always while wearing Crocs. It might be a good idea to invest in some sturdy boots to wear instead, don't you think?

Do you remember watching cartoons as a kid where one of the characters stepped onto the tines of a rake and the wood handle reared up and smacked them in the face? It happens just like that in real life, too. Not only am I a pro at stepping on rusty nails, I've managed to step on rakes too, more than once. And yes, before you ask, the handle *does* fly up and smack you in the face. Right in the center of the forehead, as a matter of fact. No need to try it yourself, I've already tested the notion a number of times. Never on purpose, of course.

The worst thing I've done in terms of pain and utter stupidity was when I needed to add fence posts to the pasture when I got my first alpaca, Carbello. Several years prior, before the minis moved in, I'd hired a professional fencer to come out and install wood posts and electric fencing to enclose a three-acre area for the minis. To save his customers money on installation costs, this fencer allowed the farm owner to help install the fencing. What that meant for me was he let me drive his truck all over my pasture, stop it where he indicated, and then watch as he employed a hydraulic fencepost driver, conveniently attached to the side of the truck, to pound the four-inch round wood posts into the hard-packed ground. I had a great time, and saved money too.

Since the minis are barely three feet tall, he only strung three lines of electric fence wire, with the top wire maybe four feet off the ground. Once I got Carbello, I worried he might be able to bound over the top of it, particularly if he panicked while being chased by a hungry coyote in the middle of the night. Realizing I needed to raise the height of the electric fencing because the wood posts weren't tall enough, I figured the only way to do it was to pound in metal fence posts next to the wood posts, then string two more lines of electric wire above the existing wire.

I bought eight-foot-tall metal posts and a heavy cast-iron fence-post driver and hauled it all home in the back of my Jeep Wrangler. Calling my brother, I asked if he could help me install the posts soon. I knew he had a clue how to do it, and I didn't. He sighed and said, "I suppose." Having known him my entire life, I really shouldn't have been surprised that weeks passed and he hadn't yet come over. Going trap-shooting and other worthy pursuits took precedence, I guess.

Finally I got fed up and resolved to figure out how to do it myself. *Big mistake.*

Since the posts were way taller than me, I couldn't figure out how to pound them in. Thinking I was smarter than a fence post, I loaded the posts in the back of my Jeep along with my trusty sledgehammer and a tall ladder and four-wheeled out into the minis' pasture. That part was fun.

Parking next to the first wooden post, I set up the ladder and put a metal fence post next to it. Grabbing the sledgehammer and heavy fencepost driver, I clambered up the ladder, grabbed the metal post, and positioned it next to the wood post. I'm not sure why I felt the need to place them directly next to the wood posts. Matters would have gone far more swimmingly for me had I not.

I heaved the metal driver up above me—it weighed a ton—and placed it atop the metal post. The drivers have metal handles on each side that you grasp and then you lift it up and then smash it downward onto the post repeatedly until the post has gone deep enough into the ground. It all went well for the first five or six posts and I was feeling proud that I'd figured a way to accomplish the task. Like so many other things I do around here, I was doing it the redneck way, but it was working.

After each post was successfully set, I would hop into my Jeep, fire it up, drive to the next wood post and repeat the sequence. Reaching the far back corner of the paddock, I once again climbed the ladder, placed the metal post where I wanted it, set the driver over it and proceeded to slam it down. I'd made maybe three up-and-down motions with the cast-iron driver when it happened. I don't know if I wasn't paying attention to what I was doing or what, but somehow my right hand came off of the driver's handle and landed on the edge of the nearby round wooden post. This all happened in a split second while the driver was on its downward trajectory.

Yup. The bottom of the metal driver smashed down onto the top of the wooden post right where my right thumb conveniently happened to be awaiting it. It split my thumb wide open, like an overcooked hot dog. Whenever I've managed to really hurt myself, it's weird how time seems to run. It's like it runs slower or even backwards. I *knew* what was about to happen, but it was all in slow-motion, and I couldn't do a thing to change the outcome.

I think I immediately went into shock. I know my thumb hurt like hell and blood was cascading everywhere. I threw aside the metal driver, leaped from the ladder, and sprinted to the Jeep, holding my right hand with my left. Jumping in the Jeep, I had to reach through the steering wheel to turn the key to start the engine, fumbling with it in my haste. Unfortunately for me, the Jeep was a manual 5-speed, and I had to reach across my body to use my left hand to shift, too. Firing up the engine, I rammed the transmission into reverse and gunned it. I promptly slammed the back of the Jeep into a small oak tree. Forward, then reverse, in a total panic. The space between the trees wasn't wide enough to turn the Jeep around—I had to back up the entire way. And let me tell you, it was a *really* long way. I held my right elbow bent, with the hand held up. Blood dripped everywhere.

Somehow I made it to the house, staggered out of the Jeep and ran inside, where I wrenched open the freezer and grabbed a bag of frozen vegetables, thinking I should try to keep the swelling down. It was far too late for that, but I was definitely in shock by that point, and things around me were getting dark, like I was about to faint. I grabbed my phone while I leaned against the countertop and then slowly slid down to the floor, where I sat in a pathetic, bloody heap. I couldn't even cry.

I dialed my brother's house and thankfully he was home. He had been just about to go out the door with his buddy to go, *where else?*, trap shooting. I told him what had happened and I thought I needed to go to the doctor. Dead silence for a few seconds, then "Why couldn't you just *wait?*" with a big sigh. Well, gee, I *did* wait. For weeks. I got *sick* of waiting. I wasn't up to telling him that right then, plus I needed him to drive me to the emergency room.

He showed up soon after, took one look at my thumb and pronounced, "You're gonna need stitches for that." Bundling me into his truck, off we went. Rather than having him haul me to the hospital emergency room, I asked him to take me to the closer Urgent Care facility. My second *big mistake* of the day.

The place was a beehive of activity—it was packed. I checked in at the front desk, holding my arm aloft, my hand wrapped in a blood-soaked towel. Trails of dried blood snaked down my forearm. The bored front desk people took my information and told me to sit and wait. I sat. And I waited. And waited. Blood continued to soak the towel. You'd think they might have decided I was a bit more urgent of a case than perhaps the guy sitting across from me who only had a nasty cold, but *nooooo*. He was led to the examining rooms before me. They made me wait my turn, as my thumb throbbed with pain. It was a long wait.

When I finally was allowed into the inner sanctum and led to a bed which was enclosed by flimsy curtains, I was told to wait, again. Eventually a nurse wandered in and took my vitals and wandered back out. The inner sanctum for some reasons didn't seem busy, at least not from what I could hear. They'd obviously kept the crowds out in the waiting room, and allowed only a select few in at a time. I sat on the bed and waited. Finally a woman doctor came in. She examined my thumb and said I would need stitches. *Duh.* No shit, Sherlock. Was your first clue the mass quantities of blood all over me? Out through the flimsy curtain she went, and I didn't see her for another half hour at least.

She managed to take the time to visit the woman in the curtain next to me, who was complaining of chest pains and related to the doctor her history of heart problems. The doctor said in a breezy manner, "Oh, you're fine. No big deal." The patient asked, "Aren't you at least going to run some tests?" "Oh, no. No need. You'll be fine." I pictured the doctor patting the poor woman on the head like a dog, then I heard the curtain being pulled open as the doctor left her room. I hope the woman survived.

I sat there. And sat there. Finally the doctor graced me once again with her presence, injecting a numbing agent into my smashed-open thumb for the eventual stitches. I don't think I need to tell you how much *that* fricking hurt. Thankfully my thumb soon went numb. Too bad she didn't inject my entire body with that stuff. I could have used it. The doctor told me she'd be back and out the curtain she went. And never came back.

I waited. And waited. I figured, *Hey, they're really busy. She must be dealing with a far more important emergency.* And then I heard two nurses outside my curtain, whispering. I moved closer to them on my little bed to hear what they were saying.

"Where *is* she?" one of the nurses whispered to the other.

"I have no idea. I haven't seen her in the longest time." the other said.

They wandered off and I was left to wonder who they meant. Soon enough they were back, and the whispering recommenced, this time with a furious undertone.

"I can't believe it. She *LEFT*." one of them said.

"*What?!* Left? What do you mean, left?" the other asked.

"She went out the door and no one has seen her since. What are we going to do?"

Now I knew who they were talking about—the doctor had skedaddled. Having interacted with her and then overhearing how she blew off the next-door patient's valid concerns about her health, I realized the doctor was a full-fledged nutcase. And still no one entered my room. The painkiller in my thumb was starting to wear off and I was becoming increasingly pissed. About an hour passed, no one came to check on me, and then I heard a new voice. A male doctor had arrived, and was talking to someone in the area outside my curtain. Wrenching the curtain open, I stalked over to him, bloody thumb and arm held in front of me and said, "I need stitches. NOW."

He looked askance at me, "You'll have to wait. There are other people I need to see."

"No, I do *not* need to wait. I have been waiting *hours*. The other doctor left and didn't tell anybody. You will stitch me up *now*." I stalked back to my bed, leaving the curtain open, staring daggers at him. I had finally gotten pissed. Why, oh why, don't I just get pissed in the first place? I'd be so much better off.

He actually listened to me. He came in my "room," closed the curtain, and looked at my thumb. As he readied to pierce my thumb with the needle and thread, I said, "Oh, by the way, because I've been waiting so long, the painkiller has almost worn off."

He looked annoyed and said, "Well, if I give you another injection, we'll have to wait for it to take effect."

Considering the caliber of people working there, I didn't trust the bastard to ever come back and so I hissed, teeth clenched, "Just sew the damn thing up already."

Yes, it hurt like a son-of-a-bitch. I didn't care. I wasn't spending one more minute in that place of horrors. I couldn't wait to leave.

When I finally made it back out to the waiting room, over five hours had passed. *Five Hours.* I can't believe my brother waited for me that long and didn't pitch a fit. He is far from patient. If he'd had any idea what was going on back there, he would have flipped. I should have flipped. At times, I wish I was more like him. He doesn't put up with anybody's crap.

I really should have reported that doctor to the Board of Medical Examiners or whatever it's called in Minnesota. She had no right to be practicing medicine. Maybe she had been hitting the supply of painkillers, had a tad too much Oxycontin, and needed a nice little nap out in her car. I'll never know. She was crazy, and that's all I can say.

My thumb took several months to heal. It was a glorious purple-and-blue mixed with black whenever I changed the bandages. I was lucky I didn't lose the whole thumb considering how hard it was smashed between the wood post and the metal driver. Have I learned anything from this? Yes. I will never use a metal fencepost driver *ever again*. I can't even look at the stinking things anymore. My stomach turns. Have I learned anything else from this? Probably not. I'll still do dumb, redneck types of things. It's my nature. Especially when people who say they will help me never bother to show up. Oh—and I will *never* walk into that Urgent Care ever again.

4

Alpaca Angst

I'd owned alpacas for well over a year, only to belatedly realize I knew nothing about how to handle them. Haltering and leading them was far beyond my skill set, not to mention actually catching them in the first place, so I went online to find local alpaca breeders and made a few phone calls. A week or two later, I visited a woman who bred and showed alpacas, and she instructed me on how to approach them slowly from the side, never head on, when haltering them. Alpacas are nothing if not skittish, so it takes time to figure out how to handle them.

Once we had caught and released several of the alpacas in her large pole barn, I noticed a female in a separate area near the crowd of ten males. The breeder told me the alpaca I was looking at was past breeding age, meaning to me she was "middle-aged." In the same penned-in area was a young female alpaca, very cute and innocent looking. I watched as the old gal simpered and trotted past the boys in an alluring manner, *Look at me, here I am,* she seemed to be saying, batting her long eyelashes and tossing her head. I felt so bad for her because the boys completely ignored her, dismissing her with a communal nonverbal look that said, *Pffft. You're old. But this hot little number here...hubba, hubba!* as they leered at the nubile young thing, who didn't have a clue what it meant to be ogled by the males, and had no idea what to do. She was so sweet and innocent and naïve looking, while the older female was trying *so* hard to be noticed. It was kind of sad. I watched the boys crowd the fence separating them from the sweet young thing, jostling each other aside in their attempts to claim her attention, and I felt sorry for the old girl.

As I watched this tableau unfold in front of me, I realized what I was seeing was *exactly* what people do. Once a woman reaches a certain age, she basically becomes invisible to men. No matter how old, how big a paunch, or how many nose hairs the men sport, they are still drawn like a magnet to younger women, dismissing without a thought those their own age. So many times in my life I've noticed older men puffing out their chest and sucking in their gut, trying to catch the eye of a younger woman—it doesn't matter what the guy looks like—fat, bald, or ninety years old with no teeth—he still thinks he can score the hot young chicks. Although women are starting to do this too, thus the term, "Cougar," which shall never apply to me, thank you very much.

Watching the alpacas made me reflect on my own experiences when, starting in my mid-40s, I got the same reaction from men as the old female did. To be honest, at first it bothered me—I was no longer considered young or relevant. Then I came to my senses, knowing that no matter what I look like on the outside, on the inside I'm still me. I looked at her in sympathy and commiserated with her, silently telling her, *I know just what you're going through, honey. You'll get over it.*

One plus of having weird and unusual livestock like alpacas was that the veterinary training program at the University of Minnesota large animal hospital conducted free farm visits as a way to field train the soon-to-be-vets. I can't recall how I found out about this, but it was a lifesaver for my budget. A group of perhaps ten veterinary students would arrive in a van with their veterinarian professor, round up my alpacas, vaccinate them, and also trim their nails and overgrown teeth *for free*. I got to know one of the lead veterinarians, Dr. McClanahan, and she later came out on her own to help me with my burgeoning herd of alpacas. She was also beginning a foray into the fiber aspect of owning alpacas, and offered to shear my alpacas for free so she could practice. At the time out in the pasture were the two mini horses, Misty and Sunny, and two alpacas, Carbello and Lombardo.

Before the sweltering heat of summer arrived, the vet and I worked together to trim the alpacas' winter coats so they didn't sweat to death. Lombardo was a suri alpaca, with long, soft white fiber. He wasn't the friendliest guy, but he grudgingly allowed us to give him his summer hair cut. Next was Carbello, a brown Huacaya alpaca. Their fiber is more of the consistency of steel wool, but softer. Carbello hated to be touched, and he cowered in the dirt, complaining mercilessly at this invasive treatment. Hearing this, Lombardo freaked out and came to save his buddy. The vet was busily shearing the fiber with her electric shaver, while I held Carbello's lead rope so he didn't bolt. I have no idea where the minis were at that point—eating hay like usual, I presume.

Lombardo took such offense at how he believed his friend was being treated—probably thinking we were killing Carbello—that he did what I had only heard about to that point: he wound up and spit full into my face. It was truly disgusting. When you hear about llamas or alpacas spitting, you might think it's only spit. *No.* Not even close. Instead, what it consists of is whatever has been fermenting in their gut—so what he plastered all over my face was a slimy gobbet of

Carbello

nearly digested hay along with a healthy helping of bile. It stunk to high heaven. I must have made some kind of tormented noise because the vet looked up from her shearing, saw the green goo all over my face, and cracked up. She could not stop laughing. I didn't think it was too funny.

A month or two later, the University vets and students came out on their annual farm visit and noticed Carbello's haircut, which to be honest, was truly awful. He was sheared close to the skin in some spots, while other areas were left long. The head veterinarian asked who had done it. When I told her it was one of her colleagues practicing her fiber-shearing skills, she roared with laughter.

5

Horsing Around

Once again the mini horses were missing in action. Over the years, they have escaped every enclosure known to mankind and this day was no different. They've trotted off to visit my brother's house, to get acquainted with the other neighbors, or just because they wanted to run off. They had to know how exasperated I was with their shenanigans. They simply didn't care.

Realizing they were nowhere in sight, and since they didn't come when I called for them in my very best whinny, I went in search of the marauding minis. I drove my car, with the dogs riding shotgun, up and down the gravel road looking for them. Coming back down my driveway, I floored it and cruised up the hill in the front yard and drove back to the pasture to look for them. I realize this may make you think I'm lazy, and you would be completely correct. It was also faster than walking all the way up there, and I was becoming concerned about their welfare. A neighbor's horse once escaped and found its way out to the highway over a mile away and was hit by a car. The horse survived. I'm not sure about the car.

Driving around up by the pole barn, through the trees I saw a truck making its way down my driveway to the house. It was my neighbor, Pat. I swung a quick U-turn and drove back down the hill, pulling up near his truck. He didn't blink an eye to see me driving all over my yard in a four-door sedan; I guess it must be considered okay in this neck of the woods. He must have thought I was giving the dogs a joyride. Perhaps he thought it best not to make any type of comment to someone so obviously out of touch with reality. Who knows.

Pat walked over to me as I sat in the car and thrust a cell phone at my face. "Do you know these two?" he asked, showing me a photo of two miniature horses grazing on grass. I assumed it was *his* yard, since he probably wouldn't take a photo of them in *my* yard.

"Yes, actually I *do* know them," I confessed, and off we drove to his house, my car following behind his truck, my dogs still hanging their heads out the back windows of my car. The minis were in full munching mode as we pulled up in front of his house. I had thought to grab one lead rope and halter, plus their usual ice cream bucket of crack (actually chicken feed, but to the minis it's like a drug) to lure them. This whole adventure was getting old.

Pat's wife Sheila came outside holding carrots which Misty and Sunny graciously allowed her to bestow upon them. While their attention was thus engaged, I snuck over and looped the lead rope around Sunny's neck to restrain her, and then was able to halter her. I didn't have a halter for Misty; she would have to remain loose.

I glanced over at Pat, who was sitting in his truck with the door open, looking as if he was finding the entire scene highly amusing. Eyeing my car, and then the two horses, he couldn't figure out how I was going to get them home. Would I leave the car behind and hoof it on foot with the horses, and then have to walk all the way back to his house to retrieve my car? He didn't say a word. He didn't have to. I knew what he was thinking.

As noted earlier, I am nothing if not lazy. Or perhaps I should reframe that—I am an expert at conserving energy. I led Sunny over to my car and turned back to Pat, "Watch and learn."

Getting into the car while juggling the lead rope and recalcitrant mini horse was somewhat of a struggle. Sunny didn't want to leave behind the carpet of succulent green grass. This neighbor is a landscaper, so you can imagine what a yummy buffet was laid out for the girls. My yard was a weedy mess compared to his. My yard was a weedy mess compared to *anyone's* yard.

Misty kept an eye on Sunny but continued to eat. Firing up the car and holding my foot on the brake, I put it into drive. My left arm, holding the rope with Sunny on the end of it, was stretched out through the open window. I turned back to glare at Sunny outside the car door and hissed, *"Walk or be dragged."* She didn't know it was an empty threat—my skinny little arm would snap like dry kindling if she dug in her hooves and refused to move. I was hoping she believed the threatening tone of my voice rather than calculating the odds of being dragged. It worked.

Off we went at a glacial crawl, Sunny in tow outside the car, Misty trotting along loose behind her, dogs in the back seat. I looked in my rearview mirror to see Pat watching with a highly amused expression. He may have taken more blackmail pictures as well.

All of us made it home in one piece, and I told the minis they were in *big trouble.* It's never made any impression at all on them in the past, but it made me feel better. I don't want to admit it, but this wasn't the first time I had used the old "walk or be dragged" routine on the minis. It had happened twice before—the minis ran off to one or the other of the neighbors and hung out eating their lawn while fertilizing it at the same time. Each time I employed the same solution in order to get them both home: lead rope on Sunny, my arm out the window holding it, and Misty trotting along behind the car. On both of the previous incidents I had managed to get us home without being seen by anyone. I can't imagine how it looked—it was highly embarrassing to be seen "walking" the horses by car, particularly because, for several years, I'd seen some people doing much the same thing with their dog. Their car would pull up on the side of the road, the back door would open, and out jumped their dog. They then followed behind it in their car as the dog ran up and down the road on a "walk." Believing this to be a stunning example of the epitome of laziness, I remember thinking those people had to be really, really weird. Yet there I was, with the mini horses, doing the same damn thing. Utter shame and humiliation.

6

BOARD SILLY

After the llama and alpacas I had owned were no longer living here, Misty and Sunny moved into their palatial garage home, to protect them from the roving packs of coyotes, and this meant the fenced pasture and the mini mansion where they all had lived were no longer being used.

One day the phone rang, and it turned out to be one of my neighbors. He had been boarding horses for extra income, and was calling to see if I would be willing to take in one of his boarders. I'd thought about boarding horses in the past, since I had enough land for it, but had wondered whether I would like having people around all the time. I thought it over and decided to give it a try. The extra income would really help, too.

Soon two gorgeous geldings moved into what was once the minis' pasture. The minis watched from their garage pen as the big boys sauntered past. Misty and Sunny had only seen big horses once before, when another neighbor's four horses escaped their pasture in the middle of the night and ended up at my house. The girls had fallen in love with them, and they fell in love with these new horses too. Kicking, squealing, rearing, bucking: the sounds of a mini horse hot to trot. I don't think the big boys had ever seen horses as small as my minis, but they seemed to think they were cute.

From their pen, the girls could gaze up the hill and see the newly arrived boys who were leaning over the fence in the big pasture, watching them back.

I set about making sure the minis wouldn't be able to get out into the pasture with the boys. I thought I could outsmart a mini horse, but I was wrong. I strung snow fence along where the old barbed-wire fence used to be, back when we had cows when I was a kid. I thought that would be enough of a barrier to keep the minis away from the big boys. Afterwards, I had let the minis out in the yard to run loose and graze, but they kept running over to the snow fence and peering through it to look at the hot guys in the pasture. They weren't tall enough to look over it. Satisfied that the minis couldn't get past the snow fence, I turned my back for a minute. I soon heard loud whinnying from Misty and turned around to see she had burrowed under the snow fence and was now standing feet away from the two big horses on the other side of their electric fence.

Sunny and Misty at the snow fence gazing with longing at the hot new guys

Having no idea how they would interact, I rushed to grab Misty before she made the colossal mistake of going under their fence, and both minis were soon back in their garage pen, gazing longingly up the hill towards the guys.

A few months later, since things seemed to be going well with having boarders, I decided to add another horse and its boarder to the mix. This was another gelding, very handsome like the others. Thankfully they all got along fairly well, although like anything else, there were some minor pecking-order disputes, and one horse ended up at the bottom of the pecking order, while another horse was the boss. Horses, chickens, people. I've seen this same stuff play out with all of them. Why can't we all just get along?

Several weeks later, the boarders wanted to have a bonfire up by the pole barn, have a few beers, and eat pizza, with their horses hanging out nearby. I was hesitant about letting them, but since I knew a water hydrant and a hose were located close by, I figured it would be okay, and joined them for a beer and some pizza. A full moon shone down that night, and the weather was perfect—a nice night to be outside. Before they left, I watched them spray water on the hot coals. I didn't think they had doused it enough, but since I didn't see any flames, I let it go and went into the house to go to bed.

At 2:30 in the morning, I woke up and couldn't sleep. I had a feeling I should get up and look out the window to see if, perhaps, a raging forest fire was bearing down upon my house. I neglected to put on my glasses, so I couldn't see up the hill to the pole barn very well. I grabbed a pair of binoculars from the kitchen drawer and went back to the window and trained them on the spot where the fire had been. There seemed to be a red glow, but I couldn't really tell through the brush and trees. I panned the binoculars around to see whether I could see the horses in the pasture, and saw a huge white-and-brown horse munching grass. Wow. He certainly looked big. I looked at him longer, marveling at how handsome he was, but then it struck me—hmmm…he seemed to be *really* close. It turns out he was. I decided to put on my glasses, and went out into the porch to look outside. *Holy crap*—all three huge horses were in my yard eating grass, fifteen feet from the house, next to my hammock. What was I going to do? I had never handled these horses—or any full-size horses for that matter—not to mention it was pitch black, in the middle of the night.

 I turned on the lights, both inside and outside, and stumbled around the house, trying to dress to go outside. My heart was racing and my hands were shaking. For once Breezy didn't bark at the noises outside. That would have been my cue to have my nervous breakdown. The boarders had assured me that they would answer their phones, anytime day or night. I called. Neither of them answered. I left panicked messages on both their phones.

 I was on my own.

 I went out the front door on my way to the car. The horses by now had meandered into the front yard near the steps and they looked at me. "Stay there, guys. I'll be right back." I drove the car up to the pasture to grab their halters and leads. No way was I going to walk through the yard in the dark with them running loose, so I drove instead. When I got the car up there, I noticed the coals had blossomed back into a merry, roaring fire, so I had to carefully back around the fire in order to get close to the pole barn door. I left the car running and the headlights on, pointing towards the house and the horses.

 I have to admit I'm scared to death of the dark, because of the coyotes, raccoons, and what-have-you prowling around out there. It used to be my favorite time of the entire day—dusk and then full dark. I loved seeing the stars, the moon. Now I'm pretty much terrified to go outside after dark. This resulted from years and years of walking out in the early hours of the morning to feed the minis, alpacas, and llama when they were in the pasture. My flashlight was continuously

So close, and yet so far...

scanning across the woods, looking for eyeballs reflecting back at me, and listening for the crunching of twigs and leaves as *something* walked across them. PTSD, that would be me.

Now there I was, up by the pole barn, completely alone, with a full moon shining above, and my flashlight shaking in my hand, scanning with it for eyes. The pole barn had no lights, but I figured out where one of the halters and lead ropes hung, and grabbed it without looking. My flashlight was still trained out towards the woods and pasture. I knew that, if I was able to get the horses to follow me up there, I'd need to have the gate open and ready to walk them through it. I didn't want to have to fumble to open it with 1,500 pounds of horse pushing me against it.

The gate was already wide open. No wonder they had gotten out. One of the boarders hadn't latched it correctly after the bonfire and beers.

I left the car there, headlights on high beam and lighting my way as I walked down the hill back to the house and the horses. Approaching them, I needed to decide which one of them I would halter. He would be the horse the other two would follow. The big paint/draft horse mix seemed to be the lead horse at the time, so, although I was scared to death, I approached him. Somehow I managed to get his halter and lead rope on him as he continued to gobble grass. And then I led him off across the lawn and up the hill toward the open gate. I was concerned that the fire would scare them, but this horse was calm. The other two horses trotted behind us as I led the lead horse through the gate. The next horse followed us in, but the third refused. He paced outside the fence as I held the first horse, as I pleaded with him to *Just come in, dammit.*

Nope. The second horse that had followed us in panicked and darted back out and the two of them galloped off. Thankfully the horse I was holding didn't make a break for it. He was a huge horse and his hooves were huge, too. I shut the gate and removed his halter and thanked him for not squishing me. I couldn't see where the other two had gotten off to, but heard their hooves thundering down the trail towards my brother's house. Running to the pole barn, I dug around for two bowls of grain to lure them with. I had neglected to bring the flashlight—it was back by the gate—so this was all done in the pitch black night—any raccoons hiding in the pole barn be damned.

The horses had made a couple of circuits by then, and I heard them galloping off again in the other direction. I knew it was now or never, and I sprinted back to the fence and darted halfway under it. I didn't want to be trampled by the big paint inside the fence, and considering how wild the two horses were outside the fence, I didn't want to stay completely outside it either. As they made another pass, I shook the two bowls of grain and called for them to come. They skidded to a halt. Food does that to a horse, especially if they know it's a treat. Opening the gate wide, I stood off to the side behind it and prayed I didn't get smashed flat. They trotted through the gate, I tossed the food dishes down in front of them then darted back outside to slam shut the gate and chained it securely closed. Back in the pole barn, I found some rope, went back to the gate, and tied that sucker shut in two more places to be sure it wouldn't open, even with a battering ram. I don't want to *ever* have to do *anything* like that again.

Back to the pole barn for hay to toss to the horses to keep them occupied, and then it was time to deal with the fire, which had gotten quite the boost from the rising wind and was now crackling merrily ten feet in the air. I reached down to turn on the water hydrant to douse the fire. The hose was no longer attached and water spewed everywhere, including on my legs. *Why the hell had they unscrewed the hose?* I thought. It took me ten minutes to get that damn hose threaded onto the hydrant because of my shaking hands. I couldn't see what I was doing in the wan light of the moon, I was worried about coyotes, and I think that may have been when I finally started getting pissed. You have to wonder why it too me so long. If the boarders had been more careful, not only with the fire, but also with latching the gate, I wouldn't have had to add to my burgeoning crop of grey hair with all the added stress.

I doused that fire like there was no tomorrow. I made a damn lake of it. Those coals and embers didn't have a chance. It took some time, but the fire was officially out. As an added measure, I grabbed a shovel from the pole barn and spread the mud and ash all over to be doubly sure it was fully extinguished. Only then did I hop in my car and drive back to my house, still shaking with adrenaline. I texted the boarders that the horses were now safe.

The next morning, one of them called me in a panic and thanked me for taking care of the problem. The other one showed up later that day and hadn't heard my voicemail or read my texts. All ended well.

7

Getting Buzzed

Because of all the lakes and swamps around here, the Metropolitan Mosquito Control workers come out periodically to test the waters for nasty types of mosquitoes—the ones that cause things like West Nile, encephalitis, and other diseases. Wearing waders, they stand near the water's edge and scoop up samples of water to look for any wriggling larvae.

If they find any, the ponds are treated with an organic substance that doesn't allow the larvae to develop into full-fledged, evil, bloodsucking adult mosquitoes. I asked them once what they used, and then checked online to be sure that it was safe for all the other various pond-dwelling creatures such as tadpoles, dragonfly larvae, fish, and turtles. It was. Their truck can be seen nearly weekly in the summer somewhere in the area, treating the ponds. Summer is a lot more bearable if you can go outside and not be instantly consumed by hordes of flying bloodsuckers, otherwise known as the common mosquito.

I don't mind seeing the trucks, but when they send out the helicopter, you know they are declaring all-out war on the nasty little buggers. The first time it happened, I heard the sound of a helicopter approaching. I thought nothing of it, since they fly over my house every so often. It came closer and closer until it sounded like it was about to crash into my roof. I was inside the house and ran to a window, wondering if I was about to be on the 6PM news. I could imagine the flashing headlines: "Woman and assorted critters found in ruins of house after Mosquito Control District helicopter veered off course. Mini horses rampaging through the neighborhood, and chickens flying everywhere. Stay tuned…more on this breaking story at 6."

Cowering as I looked out the window, I saw the helicopter fly directly over my roof at a very low altitude and head to the west, the words, "MMCD" emblazoned on the fuselage. What am I saying, "altitude"? How can flying barely fifty feet above the ground qualify? The helicopter was *that* low—barely clearing the top of the birch tree next to the house, not to mention my roof. My minis were still living out in the pasture back then, and I saw them galloping around in fear, tossing their heads, eyes wild. I didn't blame them. I felt the same way, although I am far too out of shape to attempt anything close to a gallop.

Flash forward to this summer: 8:30AM, barely morning in my book, and here it came, the deep *whump-whump* sound of its rotors coming long before I saw it. Two of the dogs were on the front steps and I looked out the window at them as the helicopter came right over us. The entire picture window shook from the rotor wash and pellets of something clicked as they hit the glass. Were they rocks thrown up from the ground? Or insecticide pellets? Then I saw the helicopter as it cleared the house and began dive-bombing one of my three ponds. Scary to watch, as it steeply dove down to drop the mosquito-killing treatment and then just as steeply immediately climbed to clear the trees surrounding the ponds. It barely made it over the treetops.

I've been outside sitting on the front steps several times when it made its appearance. One time it came screaming past from behind me and flew just above the huge red oak next to the minis' garage, executed a pinpoint 180-degree turn and came back over me. The glass-enclosed cabin was at a 45-degree angle, and the pilot's eyes met mine right before he shot past over my head. I'm pretty sure he had blue eyes—that's how close he was. I nearly raised my fist to shake it in the air like Snoopy and the Evil Red Baron.

When my brother was mowing the grass on the big hill out in the pasture for the big horses, he said the helicopter came over the top of the hill, swooping so low that it almost hit him as he sat atop the old 1952 Ford tractor. He told me the pilot's eyes went wide as he pulled up to avoid a collision with my brother.

The pilots they hire to do that job must be screened to include daredevil tendencies. I worry that one of these days the pilot will think he zigged when he really should have zagged. I hope it never happens, or if it does, he's able to set the helicopter down in the middle of one of the shallow ponds, so he has a chance to make it out alive. And that he doesn't decide to use my roof for a landing pad. He's come close enough already.

8

Feathered Fiends

Three big chickens with red feathers, all hens, moved in, for what was billed by their owner as a short-term stay: "Can you take them just until I move?" she wheedled. "It won't be for long."

Yeah, right. I should know better. This person still hasn't moved, almost two years later. I didn't have anywhere else to put them but in the Coop de Ville, the Cadillac of chicken coops, with my bantam chickens. I was concerned, since these big girls were three times the size of some of my chickens, with big personalities to match. They reminded me of roller-derby queens, shoving their way around.

The ramshackle homebuilt coop where they had lived at their previous home was unceremoniously deposited by their former owner in my driveway a few days after the chickens arrived. I guess that meant they were here to stay. One of the horse boarders saw the ugly little coop sitting by the minis' garage and asked what the heck it was, then told me, "I'd *kill* anyone who put something like *that* in my yard." I had to agree. It was ugly as sin and heavier than all get-out.

The new hens immediately asserted their dominance, bullied my little bantam chickens, and hogged all the food. They were tyrants. I

The fabulous Coop de Ville

took to calling one of them The Enforcer (I never could figure out which of their names went with which big chicken as they all looked alike), since she was a bully to everyone, roosters included. When you outweigh the boys three to one and tower over them, you pretty much call the shots. Chaos reigned in the coop. Back then, a total of twenty-two chickens lived in the coop: eight roosters and fourteen hens. I should really quit letting them hatch their eggs, as each resulting baby chick added to the teeming masses in the coop.

The Coop de Ville is big, but with the addition of the three full-size hens, it wasn't big enough. A tipping point was reached and critical mass was finally achieved. Nuclear fission was about to commence, and the feathers would be flying. The situation was stressful for everyone involved, including me. Tussles and territorial spats broke out regularly. Poor Hazel, an eight-year-old Japanese bantam, spent two months up on a ledge and didn't come down. I had to feed and water her up there.

It was too crowded, with too many roosters, too many turf wars and resultant pecking order disputes, not to mention the big hens were bullies with a capital "B." Each time I walked into the coop with food and water, I nearly tripped over rampaging chickens darting around and between my feet. I was afraid to move as I might step on one as it darted past, chased by another irate chicken, or sometimes by a whole pack of them. Something needed to be done. I, as well as all the chickens, had had *enough*.

I decided to move the three new hens, along with the worst rooster offenders, to a new coop. The eight roosters had been co-existing prior to the big hens moving in, believe it or not. The two youngest, Nigel and Alfred, decided to rock the coop and fights broke out. Not wanting to be accused by the local authorities of holding cockfights, it was time the hens and the two roosters, along with their squeezes, Lola and Bianca, found new lodgings. Two other roosters, Reginald and Aldrich, had also been acting up, attacking my favorite rooster, the elderly Filbert, so they were given the boot from the coop as well.

The ugly-as-sin small coop still sat where it had been dumped, against the outside of the minis' garage. It was too heavy for me to move anywhere other than somewhere nearby. I ended up dragging it into the minis' garage and setting it up against one of the walls. Next I went back to the Coop de Ville and popped the offending chickens into kennels and made several trips down to the garage, disgorging them from the kennels to run free in the garage with the minis. Misty hated them immediately, especially because the roosters crowed non-stop.

I never was able to figure out which of the three big hens was which, so I simply called all of them, "Hey, you." Now there were four roosters and five hens coexisting with the mini horses. It didn't go well. The gang of "Hey, yous" were still bullies, and they didn't respect the horses, either. On their way to investigate a new food source, they would dart under the minis' bellies or between their legs, and the horses would spook. I don't know how the chickens managed not to get flattened, but all of them lived through their tenure with the mini horses.

The littlest chickens, Nigel, Alfred, Lola, and Bianca, soon decided to sleep together on a wall shelf rather than in the coop with the bossy big hens. The big girls were too heavy to be able to fly up to the shelf, so the little ones were safe from their bullying. I don't know where Reggie and Aldrich slept. Since it was summer, the requisite box fans were in full force, scattered about the garage and suspended from the ceiling beams by rope, chain, bungee cords, whatever I could find. The end result was truly classy. I'm being sarcastic here.

Although I tried to hide the chicken food dish far under the coop, Sunny, the mini horse, was determined to get herself some "crack" and kept bodily shoving the coop aside to bend low and hoover up the chicken chow. She also liked to drink from their water dish and knock it over to finish things off. Finally she managed to break the water dish, probably by stepping on it. Grrr. At first, Misty was afraid of the chickens since the little ones were so hyper and flighty, flying up here and there to perch, and darting between the minis' legs from all directions. Sunny tolerated them, probably because it meant she could steal the chicken crack.

One of the big chickens, God alone knows which one, darted under her belly and out between her front legs as she ate hay. Sunny didn't miss a beat and kept right on eating. This state of affairs was not going to work, so one day I dragged the corral panels out to the front yard, latched them together to make a square pen, and brought Misty and Sunny out to mow the grass during the day. In no time at all, the grass was chewed down to the dirt, although they turned their noses up at the weedy masses of creeping charlie. Whenever they ran out of green stuff, they were sure to whinny at the top of their lungs and I would come running, no matter what I was doing, to move the pen to a fresh square of lawn. I am so well-trained.

I knew I couldn't continue to have the chickens in with the horses—Misty was on the edge of a nervous breakdown. The horse boarder who had heaped disdain upon the appearance of the small coop helped me move it out of the garage and to a new area out in the yard. For such an unrelentingly hideous structure, the damn thing weighed a ton, but we managed between the two of us to drag it over to a location near the front garden pond, under a big oak that would provide shade in the summer. We took turns hammering metal fence posts into the ground to make a small run for the chickens, and then installed chicken wire around the perimeter, zip-tying it to the posts, and then I added that wonderful innovation—plastic bird netting—above and across the entire run to keep out flying predators. We then captured the three big girls along with two of the roosters, Reggie and Aldrich, because these two roosters were actually buddies and could get along without my worrying about illegal cockfighting occurring. We carried them out to their new digs, but left the other four bantams—Nigel, Alfred, Lola, and Bianca—in the garage. I later finished the small coop by "roofing" the existing sloped bare plywood roof by hammering several sheets of corrugated plastic roofing panels onto it, and then lopping off the excess with a tin snips. This may have improved its curb appeal an infinitesimal amount, but the little coop did have a certain backwoods charm. I'm talking *really* backwoods. Now I had two chicken coops: The Coop de Ville, a chicken McMansion, and the newly dubbed Hillbilly Hotel, more like something from a rundown 1960s trailer court. After a tornado hit.

Next we tackled making an outdoor fenced-in area for the minis on the back side of the garage and up to the woods. More hammering of metal fence posts, along with digging holes for the four-inch round wood posts that made up the corners. I left that strenuous activity for my helper, since she is twenty years younger than me and strong as an ox. Then we strung three lines of electric fence tape along the entire thing. "That should be enough, don't you think?" she asked.

"I dunno…Misty is quite the escape artist and likes to

The Hillbilly Hotel in all its glory

sneak under the fence." I cringed as I remembered the many times she had run off and gallivanted throughout the neighborhood in the past.

"Even when the electric fence charger is hooked up?"

"Doesn't matter to her." I replied. I knew *exactly* what would soon happen, and really shouldn't have bothered to expend so much energy on what was looking horribly to me like actual *exercise*, which is considered a four letter word in my book, even if it does have eight letters.

We haltered up the minis and led them over to their new pasture area where they nosed around and, when Misty thought I wasn't looking, she tested the fence. The boarder's dog thought it would be fun to go in with the minis and herd them and, sporting a huge smile, he spent some quality time chasing them back and forth. The minis weren't too pleased, however. They like exercise about as much as I do. I watched as the boarder boosted up the bottom fence wire with her hand (we hadn't hooked up the charger) to get her dog back out. I saw Misty observe the dog shimmying under the fence and said, "Uh oh, Misty saw that."

"Oh, she'll be fine."

Yeah, you bet. She didn't know my minis. Her big horses wouldn't think of going under a fence. Not that they could fit…they are way too tall. Not to mention big horses don't seem to think the way the minis do. Mini horses are devious little suckers and smart as hell, and they don't mind demonstrating this fact to you at every possible occasion. Big horses seem content to laze around and munch on their hay.

We went back to work a bit more on the chicken coop. A few minutes later, I looked behind me to see Misty out and about, cruising all over the yard. Sigh. "I told you. She's really smart. She can put two and two together," I said to the horse boarder.

The boarder cornered Misty when she darted into the tuck-under garage of the house, captured her, and led her back to the fenced area. I sighed again, went into the house to get my car keys, drove the car onto the yard, raised the hood, and hooked up the fence charger to the car battery—as if I really believed this would change the inevitable.

Each time I needed to use the car, I had to unhook the battery, and make sure the minis were securely inside their garage and not free to test the fence.

One day I let them out in the morning to run around in their small pasture and went back inside the house to use the computer. An hour later, I exclaimed aloud, "Oh no! I forgot to hook the car up!" I may have slapped myself in the head as well and said, *"Duh-oh"* just like Homer Simpson does. I went out the front door and looked for the minis. Misty was still inside the fence, but not for long. She watched as I emerged from the house, and only then did she dart under the fence. It was as if she wanted to taunt me, waiting until I witnessed her in full jailbreak mode. I rushed out there and grabbed her, and soon had her back inside the fence. Sunny was being a good little mini, and hadn't escaped with her sister. Grabbing my keys, I drove the car up to the charger, then opened the hood and hooked up the battery to the fence charger. I went back inside, satisfied the problem had been solved.

When I ventured outside an hour later, I heard the sound of thundering hooves—the three big horses were galloping madly out in the big pasture. I looked out there to see they were being chased—by a tiny mini horse. Yes, Misty had escaped again, this time braving the full charge of the electric fence. I'd hooked up the charger formerly used in the pasture only because I didn't have the money to buy a new one, so I had to use the old one. The charger was a 10-mile charger (meaning this particular charger could power up to 70 acres of multi-strand electric fence) and it was hooked up to maybe 600 feet of fencing. It should have fried her to a crisp. But no, there she was, in pursuit of the big boys who seemed to be terrified of her. The tide soon turned, and now it was Misty being chased by the boys, who tried their best to kick her. Yet she managed to act the coquette, glancing behind her and no doubt batting her eyelashes, as she galloped just ahead of the stampeding trio, hoping she might be in for a little loving. Good lord, if one of those horses managed to mount her, she would be crushed like a bug. I don't think she had thought the whole thing through.

By this point, I had run up the hill and was yelling at her to get her butt out of there before she got killed. No way was I going to go in there and be trampled. They were all too wild, and I'm not confident around big horses. The minis are bad enough, and they're only three feet tall. I ran back to the house to grab my cell phone and call one of the boarders. I stammered out, *"Please can you drop whatever you were doing and come right this minute to help me?"* because I was certain Misty was going to be killed. Running to the mini garage, I grabbed her halter and lead rope along with a bucket of crack (that tasty chicken chow she loves so much) jogged back up there, and sat in a chair in the rain, waiting for the arrival of the boarder, and praying.

Misty finally tired of the chase, wriggled her fat little butt back under the fence, and allowed me to lure her with the crack. I actually think she had been having scads of fun. With her nose buried deeply in the bucket, I was able to capture her and immediately called to let the boarder know she didn't need to come; everything was okay. The big paint/draft horse was snorting and huffing on the other side of the fence, looming over it, which scared me. He's *huge*, his hooves are massive, and thank heavens he didn't realize he only had to step over the top fence wire—he would have had no problem doing it—and Misty and I would be toast. He's a very sweet guy, but she had gotten him into a total lather, and I didn't trust that it would be safe to be anywhere near him.

I later watched Misty in action as she again escaped under her electric fence. I had thought perhaps when I hooked the fence charger up to a battery, that would stop her. Nope. She stretched out her front legs, and did the horse crawl underneath. You can't keep that girl in.

9

THE DARK SIDE

Breezy is a Smooth-Coated Collie mix, and she is truly a hoot. She came into our lives one day unexpectedly. I already had two dogs, Shay and Rosebud, and wasn't interested in having any more. Two were enough. One afternoon, I went to have coffee at the home of an older woman I'd met in a networking group. Three dogs were milling around when I walked through her front door. One was her service dog, a handsome black lab, another was a small non-descript terrier type, and the other dog rocketed around the house, streaking from one end of the room to the other, bouncing up and off the couch, ricocheting around the corner into the kitchen, and back again. That turned out to be Breezy. She looked vaguely like a greyhound or whippet, but I was told she was part Collie along with whatever else made up her genome.

She seemed to be a sweet dog, but hyperactive. Somehow, and to this day I don't know how it happened, she ended up in the back seat of my car at the end of my visit and she was now mine. I remember driving away, shaking my head in confusion, wondering how in the heck I went for coffee and ended up with a dog. To clear my thoughts, I drove directly to a Starbucks drive through and ordered a double chocolate brownie. Breezy was given a dog treat and off we went, with me trying to think of how I was going to break the news to my other dogs, *Uh, girls? You have a new sister.*

Once home, I turned off the car, turned to look at Breezy in the back seat, told her I would be back in a second, and to sit quietly. Going into the house and up the stairs, I peeked my head around the built-in bookcase and said, "Girls? Can you come outside for a second? I have something to show you."

Rosie and Shay went straight to the car and waited for me to open the door to let Breezy out. It's like they already knew all about her—it was strange. I needn't have been worried about them, as the three were best friends from the get-go. Rosie and Breezy ran off to play in the yard and the elderly Shay sat back to watch with a big smile.

The next order of business was to introduce the new dog to my cats. It went well, also. Breezy was two years old and full of energy. Dog toys were quickly disemboweled and the squeaker was ripped out and tossed across the room. The toy itself was summarily shredded, with cat toys faring no better, and my old couch also took a beating. Breezy also immediately claimed prime position on the bed at night. I'm not sure how I was able to sleep at all with three dogs and assorted cats pinning me in place under the covers night after night. It was handy in the winter when their combined body heat kept me toasty warm. Claustrophobic, but warm.

Breezy has a great sense of humor, and especially likes to mess with the cats. She also has her shadow side. She loves to run off and explore in the pasture, in the regional park across the road, and at neighbor's houses. I have to keep a close eye on her, particularly in the spring and fall. Something about those times of year brings out her wanderlust. She also delights in bringing other dogs to The Dark Side, meaning she entices the other dogs into running off with her and getting into trouble. When Rosie was younger, she did the same type of thing, but Rosie never roped Shay into going with her. She was content to explore on her own, and on a number of occasions, I received a phone call from someone who'd found her and located her name and phone number on her collar tag and told me where I could find her. I installed Invisible Fencing to deal with these escapes, but sometimes her collar's battery ran low and I didn't figure it out until she had passed the boundary and took off for points unknown. I'm so grateful she never got hurt. I would have never forgiven myself.

Breezy looking sneaky

When Breezy came onto the scene, I also fitted her with an Invisible Fence collar. I don't like using the things, but if it's a choice between having a dog safe at home vs. a dead dog, I'll do it. I had to train her with the white flags in the yard delineating her allowed boundaries. Years ago when the Invisible Fencing was installed, I had told the guy to run it all the way around the yard at the edge of the woods, and also across the shallow pond to the side of the yard so the dogs could swim. Luckily he had brought hip waders to work that day.

It's not as if the dogs were constrained to a miniscule area. No, they had at least two acres of yard, plus a quarter of a pond to frolic around. Were they happy with that state of affairs? Most of the time, yes. Sometimes, though, they tested the boundaries and, if their collar battery was too low, the warning ping alerting them they were entering uncharted territories wouldn't sound. Then they knew it was time to rock-and-roll, and off they ran.

I had replaced the batteries in both Rosebud's and Breezy's collars in preparation for winter. Shay was no longer with us as she had passed that summer at the age of fourteen. I stepped to the front window to check on the dogs and saw Breezy way out in the middle of the frozen pond. When I went outside to call her to come, she refused, sitting her butt down on the snow-covered ice. Eventually I was forced to suit up in winter attire and slogged out onto the pond to where she sat. "Come on! Get to the house. You're going to freeze out here, Breezy." She looked up at me and then towards the house, but wouldn't budge an inch. I grasped her collar and got her up and moving, but then she dug in her heels. I didn't feel like dragging her the rest of the way, so I reached underneath her chest and hefted her up in my arms. She weighed seventy-five pounds if she weighed an ounce and I staggered under her weight. Good thing I work out by slinging manure and carrying fifty-pound bales of hay and sacks of chicken chow.

I soon understood her refusal to cross the pond back to the house. The snow was slushy, so my boots were wet. I now knew *exactly* where the Invisible Fence wire was located under the surface of the pond. With my wet boots contacting the icy surface while holding a wet Breezy and her fully charged collar, I experienced a prolonged zapping sensation. It didn't hurt, but it was *not* enjoyable. If you've ever held a low-voltage device and been zapped, it's like that. It's not like being jolted by the 100-volts in house wiring, although I've been there, done that myself. A word to the wise: don't ever wash the wall outlets with a wet sponge.

I whirled around, took a few steps back until the zapping stopped and put Breezy on the snow. "Wow. I don't blame you a bit for not coming when I called," I told her. Unfastening her collar, I threw it as far as possible across where the wire was submerged. She still was afraid to walk, so up I lifted her again, and staggered across the ice, all the way to the hill going up to the yard. There I dropped her, panting with exhaustion, and she ran as fast as she could up to the house and whined to be let inside. I had to go back to retrieve the collar, and then back up the hill to the house.

This whole scenario reminded me of something that happened years ago, when my friend Renee and I were in our early twenties. My parents weren't home that day. I had moved out to my own apartment by then, and she and I decided to drive out to their house (where I now live) and go ice skating. We grabbed two shovels and cleared the snow on the same pond where, thirty years later, Breezy and I were zapped. Renee and I then went back into the house to warm up and make hot chocolate, which we poured into an old thermos to keep it warm. My dad's black Lab, Niko, decided to hang out with us on the pond. We laced up our skates and hit the ice, taking time out every so often to pour a cup of hot cocoa and lace it with the bottle of peppermint schnapps Renee had so thoughtfully brought along. When the high-octane cocoa was no longer warm, we tossed the remaining liquid aside into the snow and resumed skating, more and more boisterously the more "hot chocolate" we consumed. I didn't really pay attention to what the dog was doing, not until he began staggering around more drunkenly than we were. He had been gobbling up the chocolate schnapps-covered snow—an 80-proof doggie snow cone—and he was snockered.

Renee and I weren't much better and we giggled as we lurched around the skating rink. I thought it was funny until I realized my father was going to kill me if he knew I'd gotten his prized hunting dog drunk. I had to hide him, fast. Still clad in my ice skates, I lifted poor drunken Niko in my arms and clomped off across the snow and up the hill to the house, just like with Breezy thirty years later. He weighed more than Breezy. I was in better shape back then, so I made it all the way to the house without dropping him. I deposited him in the tuck-under garage on a rug to sleep it off, and went back to the pond where Renee and the thermos awaited. My dad never knew, and poor Niko must have had quite the hangover.

Ten-below-zero with a windchill of minus forty-five degrees. Another delightful winter day. Duke's owner, Thomas came to pick up his dog to go and watch football with the "boys." I babysit Duke because Thomas isn't allowed to keep him at his apartment.. Breezy and Rosie stayed out on the front steps for a second while I was on a brief phone call. Normally when it's that cold, I put their dog coats on them, but I knew it would only be a few minutes, so I didn't. When I went to let them in, they were gone. They must have run after Duke when he left, probably thinking they could catch up to the car.

I suited up in my winter gear and plodded off to the pasture, calling for them. No dogs anywhere in sight. The big horses were at their hay bale eating, so I asked them, "Have you seen the dogs? No?" Then I got in my car and cruised down the road, scanning driveways and the surrounding woods and frozen ponds. I caught a glimpse of Breezy in a driveway half-a-mile from home. I hit the brakes and skidded forty feet on the snow-covered and icy road, then backed up and got out of the car. I opened the back door to let the dogs in and finally saw Rosie, shivering in a snow bank. Breezy held up one of her front paws since her feet were so cold. Both of them were summarily deposited without a word in the car and we drove home. I was steaming mad.

I knew Breezy had talked Rosebud into it. She had drawn her to The Dark Side. When I parked the car in the garage, both dogs were scared because they knew they were in big trouble. Rosie darted in the house first and then Breezy; both ran upstairs and cowered on the couch. The look on Breezy's face was shame-filled and apologetic, as if to say, *I'm sorry, Mom, I'll never do it again.* Yeah right, at least not until the *next* time. And that next time came only a few months later.

It was a sunny early spring weekend day. The three dogs were outside together, soaking up the rays. The next time I checked on them, only Duke remained. Breezy and Rosie were gone. Leading Duke into the house, I then did my usual routine when the dogs went missing: walked out to the pasture and called for them, walked up the driveway, calling their names. Next order of business was to jump in the car and drive up and down the gravel road, looking for them on the road, or in the woods. I couldn't find them anywhere. I went back to the house, every so often checking outside to see if they had returned. It had been over an hour and every horrible scenario you can think of had been running rampant through my mind. Rosie was nearly fifteen years old, had suffered from Lyme disease, and was arthritic. Years ago I wouldn't have put it past her to run for miles, but not now. She was too old and infirm. Plus she was nearly deaf.

The phone rang and I braced for the worst. A woman was on the other end of the line and told me she had found my dog. "Which dog? The white one, or the brown one?" I asked.

"She's white and fluffy," she said, and I knew she had Rosebud. *But where was Breezy?*

She hadn't seen another dog, but told me someone else had stopped to talk to her when she had rescued Rosie, saying she'd seen two dogs running loose through the regional park, which is thousands of acres, and tried unsuccessfully to catch them. Those had been my two dogs.

When I asked the woman where she had found Rosebud, I nearly fell over. She and her husband had been driving down a busy four-lane highway four miles away, and had seen Rosie wandering dazedly across. I am so thankful they stopped and saved her. I don't know how she hadn't been killed, other than by the grace of God. I also have no idea how Rosebud could have made it that far. Breezy would have no problem, but Rosebud? No way. Yet she had, and thankfully was still alive.

Once again hopping in my car, I drove to where she and her husband were waiting with Rosie. I bundled my dog up into the back seat, after giving her a huge hug. I was so happy to see her safe and sound that I couldn't be mad at her. We drove home and I scanned the surrounding countryside, looking for Breezy. She wasn't dead on the highway, so there was room for optimism.

Several hours later, I looked outside and there she was, curled in a tight ball under the pine tree in the front yard. I ran out to her and for once I didn't yell at her for running away, instead I bawled my eyes out as I hugged her tightly.

10

WHAT THE HAY?

It wasn't long before the horses I was supposedly boarding became the horses I was taking care of. I'm not sure how that happened, but suddenly I was feeding their hay rations twice a day, because they hadn't been fed. A hay hut had been purchased to enclose the big round bales that kept the three horses fed for a couple of weeks. When the round bale was all gone, the boarders were supposed to roll out another 1,000-pound bale and put it in the hay hut.

The latest round bale was nearly gone, and there weren't any others set aside in the pole barn. I called one of the boarders and left a voice-mail to let them know their horses were about to run out of food. Didn't hear a peep in return, so I loaded onto a plastic sled one of the small fifty-pound square bales I'd bought for my minis to eat, dragged it up to the big boys, and fed them that. They made short work of that bale. Still no response to the voicemail, so the next day I brought another of my bales up to feed them and then drove off to my job. When I came home, I saw several small square bales of hay had been left inside the pole barn by one or the other of the boarders. I never found out who. I looked out at the horses, who were milling around hayless and hungry, and I sighed. I dragged a bale out of the pole barn and fed them.

Next morning there the horses were again, lined up in a row, hanging their heads dejectedly over the fence, staring at the house, waiting for me to emerge and feed them. I took pity on them and continued to feed them twice a day, in addition to my own mini horses and chickens. I figured the round bales would arrive anytime, the boarders would put them in the hay hut, and I would no longer be on buffet duty. It didn't happen, plus there'd been no communication from the boarder I called. I continued to feed the horses because I couldn't watch them starve.

I tried calling the boarder again, and left a voicemail saying I would no longer feed the horses and that they would starve. Next morning I looked out and the horses were again staring at the house, hoping to be fed. I continued to feed them for the next two-and-a-half weeks with the square bales that mysteriously appeared in the pole barn whenever I wasn't home, but which never seemed to make their way out to the waiting hay hut.

One day I returned from work and walked up there. It had to be at least 95 degrees and really humid. Going into the pole barn, I saw a huge new pile of square bales, neatly stacked underneath a tarp. I walked out to the hay hut in the paddock, only to see it had not been filled. *Why the hell not?* I wondered. The horses were nudging against me, looking for food.

That's when I finally blew up. I grabbed the empty rope netting used to keep the hay together inside the hay hut, went to the pole barn, loaded three bales of hay inside it, and dragged the whole damn thing through the dirt and then under the fence, out to the hay hut. Keep in mind that one small bale of hay can weigh up to 50 pounds. I had *three* of the damn things in that net. Of course I was immediately sweating like a pig, and it didn't help that one of the horses tried to eat the hay as I dragged it, although I'd tossed some over the fence to divert their attention right before that. I was angry enough that for once he didn't intimidate me in the least, and I shoved him away.

A four-sided, rigid plastic enclosure, the hay hut had a number of openings for the horses' heads on each side. These things are about seven feet tall, and each side is six feet wide. Who knows how much the stinking thing weighed—over 200 pounds at least. I know that because I decided to demonstrate to the boarder that the hay is supposed to go *inside* the hay hut, not sit under a tarp in the pole barn. Not that the message would necessarily get through, but I needed to get my anger and frustration out somehow.

Shoving the horses aside as they nuzzled the hay in the netting, I reached out and heaved at that damn hut until it flipped over. The openings weren't big enough for the hay bales to be shoved through, so the whole hut had to be turned on its side first. Then the hay would be placed on the ground, and the hut rolled back up over the hay to enclose it. I had shoved the hut a bit too energetically in my rage, and it rolled over a few times. I dragged it back to the hay and batted the horses away again. They were beginning to seriously annoy me.

I got behind the hut, which was lying on its side, in order to push it up and over the hay, and was instantly rewarded with burned hands. The hut was dark grey and the side I was on was in full sun in 95 degree weather. *Of course* it's going to be incandescently hot. I needed something to use as oven mitts so I could touch it without the skin melting from my hands. I tore off my tank top and wrapped my hands in it. I probably shouldn't mention that I didn't have a bra on—it was too damn hot, and I was home alone, so who cares? Whipping off my top meant that I was standing in the middle of the paddock topless. I didn't give a rip. I was too mad, and I was also bound and determined I was going to emerge victorious over the hay hut. I'm fairly certain I wasn't visible to the McMansion on the hill, but you never know. Give 'em a show, I say. It's not like they haven't been entertained by my extensive animal-related catastrophes in the past.

There I was, completely topless, with sweat pouring off me. And I couldn't leverage that thing. It weighed too much. I pushed, I shoved, I swore a blue streak. I stomped off to the pole barn, the girls bouncing with each step, to find some type of rope. I grabbed the horses' lead ropes. Back in the paddock, I hooked them together and threaded them through two of the side windows, pulled with all my strength, but couldn't get the thing to budge. Since the hut was on its side, I needed to somehow flip it over towards me so as to get its top, at the moment positioned in front of me, to be the "roof" above the hay.

It was seven feet tall, and I had to find a way to flip it towards me without dying from it falling onto me. I probably should have given up at that point, but when I get that mad, nothing stops me. (I once carried a 250-pound car transmission up a guy's driveway and dumped it in his yard. At the time, I only weighed 125 pounds. He was supposed to be home to take it out of my car's trunk, but wasn't. I got pissed and did it myself. He never believed that I carried it myself.) Knowing how I get when I'm mad, I'd be damned if I wasn't going to get this stupid hay hut to cooperate. I stood back, wiped the sweat off my face, and thought about how to do it. I took the rope and tossed it up above me and looped it through one of the windows of the side that was high above me. Threading it down, I now held both of the rope ends in my hands. I set my feet firmly in the dirt and pulled the ropes and hut towards me. I rocked it back and forth, trying to get it to the tipping point, but hopefully not tipping onto me. I huffed and I puffed and I pulled, only to end up flat on my back on top of the netted bales behind me. Getting up, I gave it one last massive pull while screaming some *very* bad words. That finally did it, and down it came as I darted to the side to avoid being cut in two when it landed with a loud *WHOOMPH!* atop the netted hay bales. The horses came right over and shoved their muzzles in the hay. Why the hell they didn't help, I'll never know.

Bent over, my hands on my thighs, I was panting with exhaustion, chest heaving, and boobs abouncing. Sweat drenched the entirety of my body and I wiped it off with my tank top. I staggered over to the horse waterer and sat atop it, still topless, for a few minutes until I could, with any certainty, actually make it back to my house without keeling over. This time I *know* they could see me in the McMansion. I may have waved up at them and flashed the victory sign a time or two. Once back inside the house, I grabbed the box fan, cranked it to high, and lay on the floor in front of it to recover.

I'm not sure why the boarder never returned my calls and left the feeding of their horses up to me. Maybe it slipped her mind, maybe life got in the way. Eventually the round bales reappeared and it was back to business as usual, and I was off the hook for feeding the horses.

11

ANOTHER BAAAAD IDEA

On one my innumerable trips to the local feed store for supplies, I mentioned to the owner, Kim, that I was thinking of getting a goat for buckthorn removal. Believe it or not, goats love the stuff and, with the vast quantities of buckthorn choking out my woods, a goat would be in total heaven and have his work cut out for him. Buckthorn is an invasive tree that's taking over the woods in Minnesota and crowding out the native plants needed by wildlife. Goats seem to be the only animals that actually have a taste for it.

"Oh! Perfect timing," she said. "The local animal rescue has a goat that needs a new home." Out came her cell phone as she dialed and then handed me the phone. I spoke with Laura, who runs the rescue. It turned out a teenager brought home three baby goats that needed to be bottle-fed, and her dad told her *no way* was he letting her keep all of them, and she'd better find at least one of them a new home. Laura took down my contact information and said she'd have them call me later that day.

When the goat's owner phoned, she told me how me how much she hated giving up any of them, but her dad was standing firm. She had two males and one female, and she said she'd drop off one of the males at my house that evening.

I decided the new arrival would be housed with the minis. I didn't think putting him in the Coop de Ville with the chickens would be a good idea. Now I had to figure out how to goat-proof the minis' corralled enclosure. Having never had a goat, nor having any idea what they were like other than what I'd read about them, I headed down to Menard's, the local home improvement store. I wandered the aisles, making my way over to the fencing area. There I found various types of fencing material such as chicken wire, plastic snow fencing, and wire fencing. Picking up the different types, I tried to picture how I would jerry-rig it to the metal pipes that made up the minis' corral panels. I also needed to find something the goat wouldn't injure himself on, or stick his head through and suffocate himself. Finally settling on the wire fencing, now I had to decide what height to buy. I had no idea how big the goat would eventually be, but I had read goats can get out of just about anywhere, so I went for the five-foot-tall fencing, which would make it nearly as high as the top of the corral.

Arriving home, I laid out my supplies: a roll of wire fencing, tin snips, and my old trusted stand-by, zip ties. The minis watched with interest as I unrolled the fencing and attached it to the outside of the corral with the multi-colored zip ties. I particularly liked the neon green and hot pink ones. Ah yes, another of my projects that would look incredibly well-thought out and impeccably executed. The far side of the corral was the most time-consuming, as I had to step on the accumulated pile of manure I had thrown, shovelful by shovelful, over the top of the corral. Remind me why I thought it was a good idea to wear Crocs and walk on manure. Yuck. Finally the corral was suitably goat-proofed. Next I needed to do a quick clean up inside the corral area for the soon-to-arrive toddler goat. Manure was slung with great gusto over the top of the corral onto the ever-growing pile outside—

the one I had just been sinking into with my Crocs. My lightweight foam footwear definitely was not up to the task.

I had barely finished when a truck made its way down my driveway and pulled up next to the minis' garage. Out stepped a girl who looked to be around seventeen. The goat was standing quietly inside a plastic dog kennel secured in the bed of the truck. I helped her lower the kennel to the ground, she opened the door, and the cutest little goat I have ever seen tentatively emerged. Okay, so I've never seen a baby goat before. He was still cuter than anything. His coat was off-white, with brown-and-black markings on his head and forelegs. He was only five months old, and was incredibly friendly and sweet. I asked her if she had named him. "Oh yes, his name is Donald. You can rename him if you want."

I burst out laughing and practically fell on the ground, with tears coming from my eyes. "What's wrong?" she asked, probably thinking I was having some type of seizure.

"Nothing. It's perfect. His name is *perfect!*" I said, still laughing my butt off. "My brother's name is Donald. And he's stubborn as a goat, so this is absolutely hilarious to me. *I can't wait* for him to meet Donald the goat." I may have laughed in an evil manner right about then because I like to mess with my brother. He can't figure out why I continue to accrue animals, as he doesn't really have any interest in them and thinks they take too much work. He does have a point—they really *do* take work. He takes after our mom that way. Her excuse was that she grew up on a farm and had to take care of all the livestock, so once she moved away and got married, no way did she want to do that anymore. I'm sure she's up in heaven, looking down, and shaking her head at my little hobby farm and all the shenanigans that occur, perhaps muttering, "I could have told you so…but you wouldn't have listened. You were always so stubborn." Kind of like my brother.

I kept Donald as the goat's name, and I also call him my "Buckthorn Removal Starter Kit." Before the goat's owner left, we walked with the goat to the edge of the woods. I grabbed a branch of buckthorn, pulled it down to his level, and tested whether he would actually eat the stuff. He gobbled it up. I was sold. He was moving in. Cuteness factor aside, he was a buckthorn killing machine. You've gotta love him for that because buckthorn is nigh impossible to eradicate. If he could eat it into extinction while also fertilizing as he went, life would be good.

We put Donald in the garage with the minis and I stood inside with them as his previous owner drove off in her truck, waving good-bye to Donald until she was out of sight. I looked down at Donald, who was gazing adoringly up at me, his new owner, then I looked over at Misty and Sunny, who were staring at him in perplexity, wondering what manner of creature I had gotten *this* time. They'd been through my alpaca phase. Then they had to put up with the llama, who moved in as a toddler and took to suckling Sunny. He continued to do that into adulthood, and she was not amused. Later a flock of chickens was foisted on them and made their lives miserable. Now a new type of animal was sharing their digs. They looked at him askance, probably

Sunny mothering Donald on his first day here

hoping I'd take the baby goat into my house instead of theirs.

Donald was none the wiser and toddled up to the minis, making little goat noises, and looking all-around adorable. Misty tends to have a short fuse, and prefers to maintain her personal space at all times. She tried to nip at him, and I stepped in to tell her no. "Donald is a baby. Don't be mean to him. And you sure as hell better not hurt him. He doesn't know any better." She looked

Donald the goat

at me with what seemed to be a frown and turned her back on him, possibly deciding if she couldn't see him, maybe he didn't exist.

Deciding that food is the solution to all manner of problems, I put down hay in three separate areas so that each mini horse and the baby goat had its own pile of food. Misty ate from her pile, went over to shove Sunny out of the way and grabbed a mouthful from there, and then went to Donald's little pile of hay, pushing him away with her snout. He made a little mewling noise and moved off to the hay that wasn't being claimed. Misty soon claimed that pile, and on it went until the hay was gone.

The next morning I went to the garage to feed everyone, worried that Misty might have committed goaticide sometime in the wee hours of the night. I opened the door and peeked in to see Donald thankfully still alive and as cute as ever. It took some time, but now Donald has fully integrated into the minis' herd. He made a few plays for the alpha spot, but Misty soon let him know who was boss. Sunny took to mothering him, so at least he had one mini in his court.

Donald the goat seems to be smarter than the dogs. I can't tell you how many times my arms have nearly been pulled from their sockets while walking my dogs, particularly Breezy. She won't listen. She yanks me to and fro, from one side of the road to another. The minis do better walking on a lead than her. I decided to see how a goat would do walking on a leash. It couldn't be any worse than Breezy.

Not having any type of goat collar, I removed Rosebud's to use on Donald. I had to wrap the collar twice around his skinny, long neck. He wasn't sure what to think about having a collar on, but allowed me to do it. I attached the leash and we made our way out of the garage. Looking up from her pile of hay, Misty noticed that Donald was going for a walk. She lurched into action and barreled for the door, because she likes going for walks, too. I barely got Donald's butt outside and slammed the door shut before Misty could make a break for it. I'd never be able to catch her. I've been down that road too many times before. Literally down the road. Chasing minis.

It took a few minutes, but Donald was soon walking around the yard with me holding his leash. Breezy bounded up and leaped on him to play. She fell in love with Donald the first time she saw him. The two of them play, although I don't think Breezy really understands what Donald is doing when he rears up and then headbutts her. I keep telling her to wait until he's full grown and see how much fun it is then. Donald and I went over to the woods so he could munch on buckthorn. He could be out there for the next 850,000 years, and he would still have buckthorn waiting for him to devour. The woods are choked with it.

Things had gone so well that the next day I took Donald and Breezy, both of them on leashes, on a walk up the driveway and out onto the gravel road. Donald aced it. When a car went by, he was a pro. He didn't flinch, he didn't bolt, but he did stop every so often to eat leaves. He's a goat. I let him. Breezy, on the other hand, yanked me back and forth until I felt like my head was about to detach from my body and tumble to the ground.

Eventually we wandered into the regional park and walked along on a trail through the woods. Here again Donald did better than Breezy. He maintained focus and trotted smartly along on my right side. Breezy was supposed to be on my left, but of course she was instead all over the place, as was my poor arm. Three times we were stopped by people walking on the trails. "Is that a goat? Omigod it's soooo cute!" Donald graciously allowed himself to be petted and have attention showered on him. He posed calmly for photos, while Breezy actually let *him* be the center of attention, and not *her* for once in her life. Donald was only five months old, I'd had him for only a week, and he already knew how to behave. Breezy was eight years old and I'd had her for years. Either goats are smarter than dogs, or Donald was genius level—the Einstein of goats.

I sometimes let him run loose in the yard and he stays close to me for the most part. If he wanders around the corner of the garage to nibble on something, all I have to do is call, "Donald!" and he comes running. The damn goat is smarter than the dogs. What am I saying? The damn *chickens* are smarter than the dogs. Or else they listen better.

Donald was leashed on a stretchy alpaca lead rope left over from my alpaca days, and the leash was attached to a small tire to hopefully keep him from bolting off. He could easily move it and, if he did run, he wouldn't break his neck. He happily devoured grass, weeds, and the wild black raspberries. He eventually made it over to my hosta garden and I repeatedly had to get up from my patio chair and move him and his tire away, as he was swiftly decimating them. He is nothing if not stubborn. Duh. He's a goat. Why would that surprise me?

Breezy ran up and wanted to play; Donald obliged by rearing and headbutting her. I had gone back to my chair to read. Donald whined for attention, so I went over to sit in the grass next to him. Any time I walked off, he whined, and I returned. I am so trainable. Misty and Sunny were stuck in their pen and I heard Misty's loud whinny. She was jealous of Donald being out, and not her. Eventually Donald became too annoying so I brought him back to the minis.

One day after mowing the grass—a much-heralded affair, as it happens so rarely—I gathered up some of the freshly mown grass and tossed it into the corral to placate the minis. I walked around to the service door to go in and Breezy followed me into the minis' garage. She wanted to play with Donald. Normally Misty and Sunny don't mind Breezy being near them, but it seemed Misty's maternal side had emerged once Donald entered the picture. I'm not sure if she thought Breezy was planning to hurt Donald or what, but she lunged at the dog and nipped her in her flank. That had to hurt. Breezy squeaked in both pain and disbelief and ran to the door for me to let her back outside.

I walked over to Misty and had a word with her about not biting the dog again. "I know you were trying to protect Donald, but Breezy would never hurt him." Misty looked embarrassed and ashamed. Yes, horses *do* have expressions, and if you're around them enough, you're able to read their body language. Although, most of the time, their expressions tend towards, "Feed me. *Now!*"

A coyote was howling once again somewhere nearby. Glancing at the clock, I saw it was only ten in the morning. I snarled, "*Really?* Don't you damn things have something better to do? Like actually sleep when you're supposed to?" This coyote was obviously a non-conformist and was rebelling against his normal nocturnal nature. Predictably, Breezy ran to the window, looked out, began barking, and wouldn't stop.

Ignoring her to the best of my ability, I went outside later to feed the animals, walking past the chickadees clamoring at the feeder, demanding that I fill it, *now*. Fine. I went back inside, grabbed the bag of birdseed and filled the feeder. Finally back in the house after pretty much feeding every creature in the five-state area, I happened to glance outside and caught a glimpse of a large, brown shape. An involuntary gasp and a few skipped heartbeats later, I realized that no, it wasn't a damn coyote—it was a deer, moseying around the side of the house in broad daylight, on its way to feed from—you guessed it—the bird feeder I had just filled. For the birds. Not for the damn deer. Had it been spying on me from the edges of the woods, hoping against hope I would replenish the tasty sunflower seeds?

There seemed to have been a veritable stampede of deer making a run on the bird feeder the night before, judging by the copious amount of deer tracks I saw in the snow, coming from all directions and homing in with laser precision on the lone bird feeder. No wonder the chickadees were always crying piteously for food—the rampaging herd of deer had eaten all of it the night before.

Several chickadees and a nuthatch winged in, complaining loudly, and landed near the deer, who by now had her nose deep in the seeds, gobbling them up. Then I saw the other deer—a small one, I guess you could call it a teenager since it wasn't yet full grown. It was skittish and afraid to come closer. I stood motionless in the living room watching both deer, and laughing at how angry the birds were. They almost had their beaks on their breakfast, but the deer was on it before they had a chance to dig in. The big deer was completely engrossed in her breakfast, but the small deer had noticed Donald the goat and the minis, who were in their pen down the hill, busily devouring their hay. Donald in particular was fascinated by the deer, probably thinking they looked vaguely goat-like.

Donald was again in the backyard single-handedly removing every single hosta in sight. He noticed Breezy and I hop into the hammock and he came over to investigate, shoving his snout in my face, and licking my nose. Moments later, he clambered up into the hammock on top of me. Breezy launched herself off and sat a few feet away, glaring at Donald, *Hey! That's* my *hammock. Who do you think you are?!* She was aghast. Appalled. Incensed at his audacity.

My reaction was more along the lines of, *What if he poops on me?* since he tends to do that type of thing with wild abandon. Poop, that is. He's never done it on me—yet. I don't know if he knows when he's doing it, and I certainly didn't want to find out. I leaped off the hammock soon after Breezy, and Donald was forced to make a four-point landing on the ground, and scampered off to cause more havoc.

12

BOUNDARIES: WHAT ARE THOSE?

Years ago, in addition to two miniature horses and chickens, I also had three alpacas and a llama. I've always loved llamas and couldn't wait to have one, visiting the "Llamapalooza" event at a fairgrounds in early May with my sister-in-law, where we saw llamas that were trained to pull a cart. I turned to her and said, "I'm going to get a llama and then we'll hook a cart up to it and cruise down the road to the VFW for a couple cold ones." I'd seen horses tethered outside that local watering hole, so why not a llama? Gail loved the idea. I eventually did buy a llama, who was named Churchill, but never did find the time to train him with a cart, which was probably a good thing, particularly if adult beverages would be involved.

After several years of interacting with the alpacas and the llama, I realized I much preferred alpacas. Sweet and docile, they never pushed their boundaries with me. Churchill, on the other hand, delighted in it. With that, he joined a long line of others of my critters who have believed themselves superior to me, and have done everything in their power to drill that fact into my thick noggin.

The mini horses are a case in point—Sunny was two years old and

Misty was only one when I bought them. I knew nothing of how to care for or train a horse, mini or full-size. As a child, I devoured stories about horses: *Black Beauty, Misty of Chincoteague,* and another book, which I still have, depicting every breed of horse known to man. I loved the Appaloosas and Palominos, and daydreamed about the day I could have a horse of my own. My parents refused to consider it, although we had plenty of pasture land for a whole herd. I had to settle for the beef cattle we pastured for a local farmer when I was nine years old, heading out daily to find them, dodging cow pies in my bare feet. I was fearless around them and remember pretending the cows were horses, draping myself over their backs, wishing I could ride them. One of those times, my father saw me and yelled, "Good Lord, *what are you doing?* That's a bull!"

I turned to him and said, "He doesn't mind if I lay on him." The bull turned his massive head and looked back at me, stretched out across his back. He *didn't* mind. And he didn't kill me, which by all rights he probably should have.

This type of thing is a life-long behavior of mine. When I was about three years old, my mom and I were visiting at the neighbor's house. She and her friend, Donna, were standing near the pole barn chatting while three horses stood inside their paddock near the fence. Already madly in love with all things horse-related, I toddled over to them. They bent way down to nuzzle my hands, and I could swear they were telling me, *Let us out. Let us out!* And so I did. Somehow I figured out how to open the gate latch, and then fell backwards onto the grass as the horses pushed their way out. I'm lucky I wasn't squished, but they didn't step on me. Donna reacted immediately and ran over to save me and round up her horses and lock them back up in their pen.

Knowing my own history and of course fully ignoring it, when I got my mini horses, I was ill-prepared to deal with their foibles. Wanting a full-size horse but becoming more intimidated by them the older I got, one day I saw a flyer on the bulletin board at the feed store advertising "Mini horses for sale" with photos of incredibly cute little horses running about with their manes flying. *There* was the solution—I could start out small and work my way up to the big horses!

I called the number on the flyer and soon drove to a farm south of the cities where hundreds of miniature horses were pastured. It was heaven on earth. My horse addiction was in full swing and I couldn't wait to buy one. The horse breeder attempted to steer me towards suitable choices, and I chose Sunny. I knew she needed a friend, and scanned the milling herd for another mini. Meanwhile, a small grey mare walked up to me and Sunny and stared into my eyes. My choice was made for me and Sunny and Misty were delivered to my house soon after their new pasture area was fenced in.

The next morning, I peeked out the window to see if I really *did* have horses…and there they were, coming down the path towards the fence facing the house. It was a dream come true. At least it seemed that way, at first. Since it was summer, I had been told it was important to clean up the manure piles so flies wouldn't breed. Not only would the minis be chewed up alive by swarms of biting flies, the threat of disease and other nasty parasites brought by the flies were a concern. Pushing the heavy old wheelbarrow around the pasture and shoveling up manure wasn't my favorite thing to do, particularly when it was hot and humid. Once the wheelbarrow was full, I lugged it out through the gate and dumped it far away. Over and over I did this, day after day. It was a good way to get my exercise. Too bad I *hate* to exercise, and I truly *detest* being sweaty, so my mood tended towards crabby while doing it.

The minis and I hadn't yet become completely comfortable with each other. I had a fear of being kicked; I realized their hooves might hit me right in the kneecap since they were not very tall—only 31 inches at the top of their backs. Horses can smell fear and, although a prey animal themselves, they are not above messing with someone they view as beneath them in the herd. Yup, you've got it—that would be me—low horse on the totem pole.

Several times in the rocky beginnings of our relationship, I would be busily shoveling manure into the wheelbarrow and glance up to see the minis galloping full speed at me, only to veer off at the last possible second. I learned never to turn my back to them. I couldn't figure out why they were doing it. One day at work I was talking to someone who actually knew something about horse mentality and I realized the minis were asserting their dominance by charging at me. Good lord. As their owner, I was supposed to be the alpha mare, and they were telling me, in no uncertain terms, that I was the lowest of the low. Imagine how *that* made me feel—two miniature horses, barely out of toddler-hood, and they were my superiors. I resolved to right matters, posthaste.

The next time they tried their little schtick, I was ready. I saw Misty conferring with Sunny across the paddock, and it looked like she was telling her, *Let's mess with her! It's fun.* Having come to a consensus, they galloped together towards me, gaining speed. I dropped the shovel and ran straight at the lead horse, Misty, and kept running even though I feared we would collide. It worked, thank heavens. Misty's eyes widened as she realized I meant business. She and Sunny turned tail and galloped in the other direction while I chased them for another twenty or thirty feet. This scenario was repeated a number of times in the following days until they finally got it. I was the alpha mare, not them, and to be certain they completely understood, as I chased after them I yelled, "*I'm* the boss, you little monsters! *Not you! ME!* And you had better not forget it!"

After having asserted my dominance over the mutinous minis, I hoped I'd never have to go through that type of thing ever again. I was wrong. Enter Churchill the llama. He was six months old when I added him to the herd of mini horses and alpacas. He was so cute that I couldn't keep myself from petting him and giving him a hug or two. It was such a refreshing change from the standoffish alpacas. It was also a huge mistake. Again, I was woefully unaware of llama mentality, and I was unknowingly setting myself up for future problems.

As Churchill matured, he was no longer the cute, little, easily managed animal he had been when he arrived here. As llamas go, he wasn't at the top end of size and weight, but, at over 400 pounds when fully grown, he was far larger than the alpacas, who topped out at between 150 and 175 pounds. I had previously visited several alpaca farms to learn more about how to handle them, specifically how to catch the little suckers when they needed their vaccinations. The llama breeder where I bought Churchill taught me how to vaccinate an uncooperative llama. However, I was never informed about llama aggression and dominance issues.

Churchill when he was a sweet, innocent baby llama

Churchill never attacked me, or tried to stomp me to death, which I later learned from a large animal veterinarian *has* happened. What he did do was more subtle and difficult for me to put my finger on. I knew *something* was off about the way he interacted with me, but I didn't know exactly *what*. Once again, like the minis, through his actions and behavior, he was informing me that I was far beneath him in the llama pecking order. First the minis, then the llama, what was next? Chickens pecking me to death?

He "orgled" at me (a type of vocalization llamas sometimes make), which is a nice way of saying he wanted to have carnal relations with me. He flipped his tail over onto his back, pinned his ears back, walked right up to me and put his face in mine—all clearly meant to show his dominant position over me in the herd. Churchill also tried to wrap his long neck around my body when I attempted to halter him. He blocked my path wherever I tried to walk, and followed me closely when I had food and got pushy with the hay when I distributed it among the animals.

I began my search online to figure out what to do about his behavior, browsing through llama breeder websites until I found the answers I needed on llama breeder Alvin Bean's website. Reading about the same types of behavior Churchie was exhibiting helped me know I wasn't the only one who'd ever had to deal with a llama invading my personal space. I sent off an email to Alvin asking for his advice on how to handle my llama.

I described the behaviors and how I'd responded to them—when Churchill orgled at me, I had reprimanded him by saying "NO!" and bopping his nose. Turns out I had responded exactly as I should have according to Alvin, as a method of correction for Churchie to learn to respect me and my space. He suggested I focus on boundaries and making sure I immediately corrected the llama whenever he did any of the behaviors within arm's length of me. He said he uses a tennis or badminton racket to bop his llamas on their noses. As far as getting Churchill to allow me to catch him so I could halter him, Alvin told me to invite him into my space by bending towards him like I'm going to sniff noses with him. This seems to be the llama equivalent of a polite handshake. Churchill would learn this was his cue it was okay to come into my space. Otherwise, llamas should be backing away from us as we go about our business, and only approach when we invite them to do so. I had no idea llama etiquette was so arcane and involved.

Armed with this valuable information and knowing that Alvin had my back, even if he did live thousands of miles away, I was ready to teach my llama (and myself) the meaning of "boundaries." Marching out with new purpose to the paddock, arms full of hay, once I got to the fence, I announced to the waiting minis and llama, "Ok, Churchill. I've got you all figured out and I know what you've been up to." He looked at me and I swear he batted his long eyelashes at me. "Don't act so innocent...you knew *exactly* what you were doing. And I refuse to let you boss me around anymore." I tossed the hay over the fence and watched them dig in while I planned my llama boundary enforcement countermeasures.

Once they had eaten their breakfast, I climbed over the gate—yes, I could have simply opened the gate, but it was far more fun to climb over it—and entered their domain. Since the path up to the mini mansion (their three-sided, slapped-together-in-a-ramshackle-manner plywood shed) was where most of Churchill's mischief towards me took place, I headed on up the path. Churchie immediately moved to block my way, turning his body so he was sideways across the entire path. He turned his face towards me with a sneer that said, *What are you gonna do about it, huh?*

This, I thought, *this is what I'm gonna do about it, you snotty llama!* and I walked straight up to him, put my arms out, and shoved his torso as hard as I could. At that time he wasn't yet at his full weight of over 400 pounds, but it was still like trying to move a mountain. I dug in my heels in the dirt path and shoved him some more. "MOVE!" I yelled. "You are *not* going to win. I don't care how many times I have to shove your damn body, *you are not going to win.*" I bopped him on the nose with my fingers several times to reinforce my message.

Eventually he realized I was serious, or perhaps he simply tired of my slamming ineffectually into him, and he moved out of my way. I'd learned that, if a llama blocks your path and you walk around him rather than making him move to allow you to pass, he will think he won, which in his mind means he is dominant and you are to be considered as less than llama droppings. No way was I going to settle for being manure any longer. I had battled the minis and asserted alpha mare-hood, and I was damned well going to be top llama. You'd think those ungrateful beasts would have a tad of respect for me, after all, I was the one who bought their hay and cleaned their paddock. Although, to them, it may have looked like I was their hired maid and domestic servant. Animals. Who would have thought they were capable of so deviously training their humans to do their bidding?

Churchill proved to be a stubborn llama, and I had to repeat the same thing over and over, especially when I walked up that path. He kept trying to wrap his long neck around me as well as walk into me, pretending he didn't do it on purpose, and he also was pushy when I had his food. I wasn't afraid of him because I didn't believe he would turn truly aggressive and rear up and stomp me. It wasn't like that at all—more that he had no respect for me and wanted to let me know it at every opportunity.

I realized belatedly that this whole situation was the exact thing people do to each other. If you don't let other people know they have crossed your boundaries, they will continue to do it and walk all over you, and have no respect for you. You have to first tell them to back off, and if they don't, follow it up with actions, letting them know in no uncertain terms that you will not put up with their behavior. My having to go through this with animals shone the light on how I've allowed people to do the same thing to me, and that, with people or animals, it needs to be addressed immediately or it gets worse. I suppose I should thank the animals for this lesson but, just like with new people who enter my life, I need to continually mark out my boundaries.

Donald the goat is a case in point. When he came to live here with the mini horses, he was barely five months old and cute as could be. He also knew how to wrap me around his little cloven hooves, gazing into my eyes with what seemed to be adoration. Not having learned my lesson with a baby llama several years prior, I was repeating the same mistakes. Two months into Donald's residence here, I realized the goat, rather than adoring me, was instead grooming me to be bottom goat. The minis, particularly Misty, strictly enforced their boundaries with him. Whenever Donald got too bold and tried to scarf up the best bits of hay, Misty would nip at him and run him off. She was telling him to back off, and to respect her as the boss of the herd.

Breezy, the dog, loved Donald and would play with him whenever I let Donald run free with her in the yard. The goat invariably stayed close to us, so I wasn't worried about him being eaten by a coyote passing through at two in the afternoon, as they are wont to do around here. I've always wanted a goat for some reason, so I loved watching Donald's antics. At a young age, he exhibited typical goat behaviors such as rearing up and butting at Breezy when they played. Breezy thought it was fun, but I reminded her that Donald would eventually be bigger than the minis, so she might want to think about how much fun it would be to be rammed by a full-size goat when he grew up. He had come to us already wethered (neutered) and his horns had been removed, so I didn't have to worry about mating behaviors or being impaled by a stray horn.

Watching Donald rear up and ram Breezy was one thing. When he tried to do it to me, putting his front legs up on me whenever I turned my back on him, my first thought was, *Not again*. I knew I had to discourage his behavior immediately. Going online was no help, as no one really addressed this problem with goats as they had done with llamas. I was on my own.

The next time it happened, I was in the minis' garage shoveling manure. As I lifted the shovel, loaded with manure, to toss it over the corral panel, Donald sidled up behind me and jumped up, putting his front legs on my back. I whirled around,

Donald on the raised flower bed, being a typical goat

dropping the manure back onto the pile, and pushed his legs away. He tried it again, this time face-to-face. "No!" I told him, and pushed him away again. Those sweet brown eyes looked into mine, this time in a calculating manner, rather than the supposed adoration. Donald was a fraud. I had thought he was a sweet little guy, huggable and pettable, but in reality he was scheming to move up in the herd's pecking order, and at my expense, as I would be at the bottom, under him, Sunny, and then Misty, who was the boss.

"It ain't gonna happen, buddy." I said. "I've been down this road before, and I will not be bested by a goat. You are *not* going to win this."

He reluctantly turned away and went back to the hay, where Misty shouldered him aside. "See?" I chided him. "You think you're such a hotshot, and Misty just told you where you really stand." Donald pretended not to hear me. The truth hurts, doesn't it, big guy?

13

Swim With the Fishes

Early one afternoon, I went to check on everyone in the Coop de Ville since the day was hot and humid. All were fine, and I adjusted their fan to high. Yes, my chickens are spoiled. Well, the minis have a fan, why shouldn't the chickens?

I had just opened the coop door and stepped outside when a lone black horse galloped up from the front yard and skidded to a halt outside the chicken run, rearing up, bucking, and snorting a few times for good measure. At first, I had no idea what was going on. The horse had appeared out of nowhere, and I couldn't figure it out. He was soaking wet with no saddle, no rider, with only his bridle and reins hanging loose at his side. It took a few seconds before I realized he was one of the horses being boarded in my pasture. But why was he running loose and alone wearing only a bridle and reins?

I walked slowly to him, my hands out, talking softly, "Calm down, it's okay. Where's your owner?" Nostrils flaring, sides heaving, he danced from side to side as I approached, and I wondered if I would be safe. This would be only the second time I had to handle and lead a big horse by myself. The first was when the three horses had escaped in the middle of the night. Not looking forward to it any more than the first time, I repeated the mantra, "Stay calm, stay calm." I was saying it more for myself than for him.

He tossed his head and rolled his eyes as I caught hold of his reins. I looked towards the driveway—the direction he'd come from—to see if I could see his owner anywhere. Nope. It was up to me to get him safely back in the paddock. I grasped his reins and led him up the hill to the gate. The other two horses were busy stuffing their faces at the hay feeder which for once had been filled. I fumbled with the gate chain, opened the gate, and led him through. That had seemed easy enough, but when I took off his bridle, he head-butted my shoulder a few times, hard. Not good, because I figured he was trying to assert dominance over me. Not to mention he outweighed me, big time.

"*No!*" I said and quickly backed out of there. Next I went to locate his owner. I had visions of her lying in a heap, tangled in the remains of a saddle, somewhere in the thousands of acres of parkland across the road from my property. I had no idea how I was going to find her. By the time I made it back to my front yard, there she was, walking down the driveway, soaking wet, her boots squelching with each step.

As she made her way up the front yard to where I stood, I mutely pointed back at the horses, still in the throes of horse-induced PTSD, and stammered, "Uh…your horse was loose for some reason, so I put him in the pasture." Turns out she had taken her horse for his very first bareback swim in one of the ponds in the park. He understandably freaked out and threw her off into the water. By the time she surfaced, he had galloped off for home. Good thing he knew where he lived. And she *laughed* about it. Horse people. They're a different breed.

The three big horses were galloping madly around their paddock, manes flying and tails streaming behind them. Soon they screeched to a halt at the fence, dirt clods flying in the air, and looked towards the house. Not knowing what had gotten them all in a lather, I decided to take the dogs out with me and investigate.

The first thing I noticed was the top fence line—a line of electrobraid, which is a flexible rope-like electric fence wire—had fallen out of its plastic holder and was now sagging far too low. Low enough that, if the boys decided to walk over it, they'd have no problem. My minis would have made a break for it already, but these guys didn't think like that; they were content to remain inside the fence with the hay bale. I'm thankful for that.

The big horses were too wild for me to consider fixing the fence from within the paddock, and so I scuttled along the outer perimeter, tripping over brush piles and getting snagged by prickly bushes. The horses resumed their wild galloping, but now the dogs had snuck under the fence and were out there with them, totally oblivious to the danger.

One of the horses galloped towards me and skidded to a stop and shoved his face over the fence right up to mine. I had no room to back away; I was trapped in front of a pile of brush. Petting his nose, I told him, "It's ok, everything is fine. *Calm down.*" They may have had spring fever, or perhaps they had spotted coyotes lurking—I had no idea what had gotten into them.

The dogs had moseyed to the far end of the paddock, over by the woods and I called for them, worried about the horses stampeding them, or coyotes lunging out at them. I'm not sure which would be worse. Death and destruction and mass quantities of gore would be the final result either way.

As the dogs turned to come back, one of the horses ran up to Duke, and turned his back at him as if to launch a kick. Duke had no idea why his buddies, the horses, were acting so nasty. Every other time he had hung out with them, they'd been best pals. I yelled for Duke to run and then saw Breezy zig-zagging her way through the gauntlet. She ran under the fence and made it out safely. The horses took off again, shaking their manes. Rosebud wandered about willy-nilly, not hearing me since she was half deaf. Hurrying to fix the fence, I turned to go back to the house, hoping the dogs got the clue and followed me.

The horses milled around, danced about, and then darted off. Duke had his head down and doggedly made his arthritic way towards safety. Suddenly, the biggest horse, the paint/draft mix, cantered up behind him and shoved at Duke's back several times with his muzzle. Confused, Duke turned to look back and saw the rest of the horses bearing down on him. I've never seen him move so fast—he skedaddled as quickly as his tired old bones allowed and under the fence he went, safe at last.

Sprinting to the pole barn, I grabbed for the closest thing I could find—the training whip I had seen one of the boarders use to teach boundaries to her horse. She never whipped him; it was more of a visual cue. Back at the fence, I waved it at the horses to get their attention on me and away from Rosie, who was still daydreaming along towards us, not paying any attention, her nose to the ground. One of the horses nearly went after her, but I yelled and waved the whip at him. Rosie made it out in one piece.

My chest was tight, I was stressed to the gills, and I'm pretty sure I had a few heart palpitations in the aftermath of all the excitement. Heading back to the house with the dogs, I lectured them the whole way that if they went out to visit the horses, to *never* turn their backs on them and to be ready to run for the hills if need be.

I later asked one of the horse boarders what could have gotten into the horses to make them act that way. Her reply? "Oh, they just had spring fever."

14

Bird Brains

With so many different types of birds and waterfowl making their homes somewhere on my land, it's no surprise when something odd happens with the birds. It's no surprise when something odd happens around here, *period*. Actually, I would be shocked if something *normal* happened. That would probably send me right over the edge of the cliff.

One morning I went out to feed the minis in their garage. Normally I toss the hay over the top of the outside attached corral, fill their water bucket, and only then do I go inside the garage to open the big door to let them out for breakfast. On this particular day, a female robin was standing atop the pile of horse manure I had heaped outside the minis' garage. She flew off when she saw me, over to the lowest oak bough above the small chicken coop, known as the Hillbilly Hotel, and looked down towards the enclosed chicken run. *Chirp chirp CHIRP!!* Since my next stop was to feed the chickens, I walked over there, wondering what she was all in a fluff about.

I knew soon enough: she was trying to tell me her hubby was trapped under the bird netting covering the chicken run. He frantically flew from the ground inside the run up to the top of the netting, about six feet up, but couldn't get out. I have no idea how he managed to find his way in there. He saw me coming and redoubled his efforts at escape with no better luck. I slowly opened the front chicken wire to give him an escape route, and stepped back, telling him "Go for it, I won't hurt you."

In no time at all, he flew out and up to perch on the tree branch above the coop. Fluffing out his feathers, he looked sheepish and embarrassed. I told him "It's ok, it could happen to anybody. I'm just glad you weren't a hawk. It would have sucked getting one of those out of there." Meanwhile, his wife continued to nag and scold from a tree close by. He's probably still listening to her complaining.

My backyard includes a small garden pond with an accompanying waterfall. Summer mornings bring all manner of birds to bathe under the cascading water. I've seen red-tailed hawks splashing about, as well as robins and assorted other small birds, although not at the same time as the hawk. Birds aren't *that* dumb. Recently I spotted a barred owl as it swooped in and landed on top of the gazing ball next to the waterfall. He may have been looking for a bite of breakfast amongst the many frogs that populate the pond, or he could have simply been enjoying the relaxing sound of the water as it traveled over the rocks on its way to the pool.

As I sat on the front step on a balmy summer afternoon, I noticed two hummingbirds perched on the tomato cages on my front patio, looking at me. They had visited the hummingbird feeder and now were taking a well-deserved rest. I looked over to Breezy sitting next to me, and said, "I really miss the hummingbird that used to buzz my head and hover in front of my face the last couple of years whenever I'd sit out here. I wonder what happened to her?"

The next morning as I sat on the step with my coffee, I heard the unmistakable high-pitched whir of a hummingbird's wings as it flew up behind me, buzzed around my head, and hovered in place in front of my face. I'm not ashamed to say that it made me so happy, I may have cried a bit. Later that afternoon, while sitting on the back patio and talking on the phone, a hummingbird flew up, hovered in front of me for a few seconds, and then buzzed off to points unknown. She somehow heard what I had told Breezy the day before, and came through for me. It brought joy to my heart.

Out in the big horses' paddock one day, while engaged, once again, in raking up manure, I saw a lone turkey vulture flying in circles above the pasture. I silently asked it to soar closer, and it soon circled over my head. Later that day, two more of them flew together above the chicken run. A few hours afterward, I saw six of them flying in formation, incoming from the east, soaring in tight circles over me as they approached the chicken run, where the chickens were pecking about. They might be called "turkey" vultures, but I bet chicken would be on the menu if they could manage it. Seeing them flying en masse towards the Coop de Ville, I dropped what I was doing and ran up there to make sure the chickens were safe.

Outside first thing on a fall morning, the dogs and I were gathering leafy branches from the forest of buckthorn to feed Donald the goat as a treat. Nearly all the other trees were already bare, their leaves inundating my lawn; a carpet of brown as far as the eye could see, with patches of green grass poking through here and there. Catching a movement from the corner of my eye, I saw a bird land in the birch tree in front of the house. I couldn't see it well between the bare branches but it looked far larger than a robin. Walking closer, I realized it was a red-tailed hawk, perched in the topmost limbs with a good view down the slope to where the small chicken coop is. I hadn't yet let the chickens out into their run, so the hawk couldn't eye what he was obviously hoping to be breakfast. He saw me and winged off to an oak tree on the other side of the house and then flew off into the woods.

Later that day, the chickens in the Coop de Ville were pecking around in their run while Breezy and I lounged in the hammock, contemplating a nap. I had set down my book, settled more comfortably on my pillow, and snuggled with Breezy under the blanket (it was only 60 degrees that day) when I noticed an osprey fly directly above our heads towards the coop. It flew straight over the chicken run where the chickens were completely oblivious, and continued on towards the pasture. I can't sing the praises enough of the bird netting I used to cover the top of the run—birds of prey wing in with great regularity, swooping in to get a chicken dinner, only to see the netting and realize they would be caught in it if they attempted to break and enter. A truly secure chicken run would instead have metal hardware cloth on all sides and the top, as well as buried around the perimeter to keep out digging predators. I am far too lazy to go that route, and instead make do with what others might consider a redneck version. Why do you think I named the other coop The Hillbilly Hotel? Because, no matter what I build, it's some seriously redneck hillbilly construction. Part of that is because I don't know what the heck I'm doing, while the other part is good old laziness and sheer ingenuity. Duct tape and zip ties are my major construction materials. It's worked for me (and the chickens) thus far, thank goodness.

A wild turkey was browsing out in the horse pasture early one morning. Later that day, while in the house, I heard a weird noise outside. Was it a chicken gargling? A Canadian goose choking on a piece of my weedy lawn? The dogs were all inside, so I knew the noise wasn't coming from them. I looked out the living room window and saw a turkey—it could have been the same one from the morning—parading down the hill in the front yard, past the Hillbilly Hotel. The chickens hid underneath their raised coop and watched it saunter past. Nearby, the minis were in their outside corralled area, having dinner. Misty glanced up from her hay unperturbed; she knew it was no threat. The turkey, noticing her, Sunny, and Donald the goat, circled uncertainly on the driveway but then cautiously crept past, putting the pedal to the metal and running full out up the driveway toward the road. Those suckers can really move when they want to. It's funny to watch their long legs and ungainly stride, with their head and necks bobbing forward and back as they run. It looks ridiculous, but I have to say, they can accelerate far faster than me.

15

Running with the Rodents

A brand new year: the first day of January. The outdoor thermometer read a sweltering 14 degrees above zero; the sun was barely cresting in the east above the treetops far across the back pond. All three dogs were outside enjoying the brisk weather, the girls outfitted in their stylish winter jackets. Duke had no need of winter attire, as his coat is far too thick. He loves the cold. I checked on them through the front window. Duke and Rosie were happily sitting in the snow in the front yard, watching for any excitement out on the road.

Breezy was standing down by the snow-covered front garden pond, ears cocked, intently watching a drift of snow. She suddenly leaped downward, buried her face in the snow, and came up with something in her mouth. She ran in circles of delight on the driveway. She dropped it and I could see it was a fat vole—similar to a mouse but with a longer nose. It ran off, and she chased it. Picking it up, she tossed it in the air. It ran, she chased it, same thing, again and again.

This game was too easy, so she scooped it up and ran with it in her mouth up and over the snow bank and into the half foot of snow in the front yard where she dropped it. It burrowed into the snow, trying desperately to hide. Breezy dug it up, picked it up and dropped it, it burrowed into the snow, she dug it up all over again and it ran. She threw it into the air and pawed at it as it came down, like a cat playing with a mouse. *The damn dog is a cat!* I thought.

I told Nutter—who is Breezy's secret cat boyfriend—to come watch. "Hey, Nutter. Did you know Breezy is really a cat? You have gotta see this." The two of us watched as Breezy retreated a few feet and watched expectantly. Wind had sculpted the snow into drifts resembling frozen waves on the ocean. The vole ran up and over a drift and back down into the trough where I lost sight of it. *There!* Breezy pounced and threw it back up in the air. Chase. Throw. Run. Dig. The poor thing was so discombobulated that it ran *towards* the dog every time. Breezy eventually tired of the game and went to sit next to Rosie. Since I witnessed no further activity, I figured the vole was dead. But no, there it came—motoring up and over the snow, appearing and disappearing like the boat fighting the gigantic waves in the movie *The Perfect Storm*.

I opened the window, which I should have done long before, and said to Breezy, "Let it go, Breezy. It showed it was a true warrior." She did leave it alone, but Rosebud didn't. The vole made it all the way up to the top of the snow bank along the driveway and somehow managed the big drop down. Considering his size, it was rather like leaping from the top of the Grand Canyon for that little guy. It launched itself into the air, made a safe landing, and scurried off. Rosie ran over and chomped on it while Breezy observed with approval. I think Rosie dealt it the final death blow because I found it later that day dead near my garage. Poor little guy.

What in the heck is making that racket? I wondered as I puttered around in the house. A metallic type of noise sounded periodically, then silence. The sequence was repeated every minute or two, and it was starting to get on my nerves. All I could tell was that it was coming from outside, at the front of the house. Setting down whatever I was carrying, I moved to the front window for a look-see. Directly below me, Breezy was pushing around the six-foot-long section of gutter downspout I had set down on the concrete patio months before and forgotten about. She shoved it a few feet, cocked her ears, and ran to the opposite end to look into the opening. Almost immediately, she ran to the opposite opening, and then pushed the gutter piece with her front feet. Sometimes it simply moved a few feet, other times it rolled over a few times.

This went on for at least twenty minutes, and I watched the whole thing play out. I think she had trapped a red squirrel inside. Breezy likes to hunker down and stalk the squirrels. She's never caught one, but lives for the chase. No doubt this was one of the evil creatures living in my attic, which had emerged from its comfortable palace and encountered Breezy. Normally the little vermin run for the trees, but Breezy must have been far too close, and the squirrel ran into the only hiding place he could find in a pinch: the gutter section.

The dog was having far too much fun, flipping that squirrel end for end. The poor thing must have ended up with a horrible headache and hours of dizziness. I was as entertained by it as Breezy seemed to be. Each time when the squirrel ran for the far opening, hoping to make a run for it and escape, the dog headed it off at the pass and then gave the gutter a flip or two, just for fun. Breezy must hate squirrels almost as much as she hates coyotes.

Eventually she tired of her game and scratched at the front door to be let in. She fell asleep on the couch and her legs were soon twitching in a dream. Probably of catching squirrels.

16

Swan Lake

Another chilly early spring morning. I decided to stay inside the house to drink my coffee rather than freeze my butt off sitting on the cold front steps, although I have been known to sit out there in thirty degree weather at times, as long as there's no wind.

I spotted Mr. and Mrs. Mallard Duck lounging in the grass where I have my hammock in the summer. Duke was sleeping on the front step, blocking the storm door with his body, so I couldn't open it. I didn't want to scare away the ducks by going out the back door and walking past them to get around to the front of the house. That meant going out with the dogs' food bowls through the walk-out basement to the tuck-under garage. The dogs gobbled up their picnic breakfast while I snuck over to the corner of the house to spy on the ducks.

Both had their heads tucked under their wings, and were snoozing happily in the wan April sunlight. Eventually Duke got up to use the facilities at the edge of the woods. I watched the ducks observe him, showing no concern whatsoever that a big, fluffy dog was nearby.

Having competed his ablutions, Duke finally noticed the ducks, but continued on back to his spot on the front steps and didn't bother them.

Later the duck couple wandered around in the backyard, checking out possible nesting spots. From inside the house, I watched them stop to eat worms or grass as they wended their way to the back garden pond. *Plop!* They hopped in and swam around, which made me laugh because it's not a big pond—six-feet-wide and eight-feet-long, with a small waterfall at the far end. They barely had time to swim to the opposite side before they had to turn around. Mr. Duck debonairly emerged and sat on one of the rocks to keep watch as his wife bathed, her wings dipping, and water droplets cascading about. They came to visit the pond for several weeks. I loved watching them. The dogs for the most part left them alone.

A few days later, I was still clad in my pajamas and slippers, although it was 7:30 AM. Actually, jammies and slippers are the de rigeur clothing choice for me at home. Comfy, warm, and who the heck is going to see me? Well, the horse boarders have. Other than raised eyebrows and significant looks to each other, they didn't say anything about my sartorial choices.

Out on the front steps, I fed the dogs their breakfast. Hearing the trumpeter swans calling somewhere in the sky, I ran to the backyard hoping to catch a glimpse of them flying overhead. I didn't see them, but could hear them in the back pond. It had rained the day before and I ran across the damp grass in my fuzzy slippers. Through the still-leafless brush and trees, far off in the pond, I spotted them swimming gracefully, trailing a wake behind them. Trying not to be seen, I found a suitable vantage spot and sat down on the damp earth on the steep hill leading down to the pond. Swans are flighty and don't let people near, so I didn't want them to see me. The neon orange slippers I was wearing might have been a problem, unless they were colorblind. You could probably spot those suckers from 45,000 feet above in an airplane.

At a size of almost ten acres, of my three ponds, this is the only one big enough to draw swans in for a swim. In awe, I watched them dip their long necks underwater, completely submerging their heads as they ate breakfast—some type of succulent pond weed emerging from the mucky depths after a long winter hibernation. The pond is shaped like a long "L" and I was at the longest top end of the "L" while they swam near the bottom corner. Silently I whispered a little prayer that they might swim in my direction so I could see them better. I waited patiently on the hill, shivering in the cold as they continued swimming and dipping their heads.

One finally swam in my direction and then the other followed. Hoping against hope they'd continue closer, I kept completely still and quiet. And then I heard crunching leaves and snapping twigs behind me. Worried it was a coyote I whirled around, only to see Duke. My spirits sank—the swans would never come any closer if they saw him. "Duke, go back up in the yard," I whispered. Nope. He chose not to hear me. Nose to the ground, snuffling loudly, he ignored me and meandered past. The swans saw him. "See the big white birds, Duke? Don't go down to the water. You'll scare them off."

What did he do? Yup. Went right down to the water's edge. It took him a while to find the easiest path down the steep terrain with his arthritic hips and shoulders. I heaved a sigh and watched, giving up any hope of a closer look at the swans. Turning my gaze from Duke's slow and painful descent to the pond, I watched, astonished, as the swans swam *closer,* until they and Duke were practically nose

Duke

to beak, ten feet from each other. He looked at them, then up at me. He turned his attention back to the swans and they seemed to commune silently for a minute or two.

My mouth was hanging wide open. Aren't they supposed to be afraid of dogs? And to top it off, a lone Canadian goose swam up to join in the moment. The swans dwarfed that large goose, so you can imagine how big swans are. I made sure to stay stock still so they wouldn't notice me, although I was hard to miss in my hot pink pajama bottoms and clashing orange fuzzy slippers. The swans and goose looked on as Duke lowered his muzzle to lap up water from between the grasses on the pond's edge. Several querulous trumpeting noises emerged from them as they gazed upon the huge white dog. They were spellbound. It was uncanny. Good thing it was early spring and the flies weren't yet out in force, because my mouth was open in wonderment and shock, and flies could have flown right in.

Duke turned away, then slowly and stiffly made his way back up the embankment, the swans and goose watching intently. He tottered to where I sat and I hugged him fiercely, tears in my eyes, as I asked, "Duke, what in the *hell* did I just see? Why were they drawn to you? I have never seen *anything* like it. Thank you." The swans had finally noticed me (hard to miss hot pink when it moves) and they slowly swam away, the goose being last to leave. Duke gave me a true gift that morning; it brought tears to my eyes and joy to my heart.

I will never forget it. Thank you, Sir Duke.

17

A Plague of Coyotes

Finally, some much-needed hammock time with Breezy. I let Rosie and Duke out of the house after their extended afternoon siestas. Breezy soon leaped off the hammock and sent me spinning off onto the ground. So much for relaxation. She took off towards the horse pasture, where I saw a dark grey shape streaking away towards the woods. *A coyote*, I thought as I ran barefoot after my dog, calling for her. Somehow I got Breezy to listen to me and come back before she hit the woods where the coyote had disappeared.

I ran to retrieve the baseball bat from the back porch. Another bat is stored by my front door—you never know when you'll be needing to bash in coyote brains. I put on my trusty Crocs just in time for Breezy to charge off again, this time with Rosie and Duke in tow. Awesome. Now I had to worry about *three* dogs being attacked. The two elderly dogs, Rosie fifteen, Duke fourteen, were leaping and cavorting like pups, so excited to be in on the coyote hunting expedition.

I ran after them. "No! Stop! Don't! Crap!" All I could think of was Breezy getting into a knock-down drag out fight with a coyote, with

Rosie and Duke, the geriatric crowd, wading into the fray, and me with a baseball bat and Crocs chasing after all of them into the thick brush and poison ivy. The dogs came back towards me then pranced off towards the woods. They were having so much fun, their tongues lolling. It was the most excitement they'd had in pretty much forever. No heart attacks among the oldsters, thank God, me included. I told Duke, "Wait until your dad is here and then you can chase all the coyotes you want." And his *dad* could deal with fighting them off instead of *me* having to do it. Finally I got the three dogs herded into the porch, stressed out and not happy at all. That would be me, not the dogs. They were having the time of their lives.

Late one night years ago, we were all cuddled up sleeping. Rosie was burrowed underneath the bed as she liked to do. My dog Shay, who has since passed on into the great dog park in the sky, and the cats slept in the bed with me above where Rosie lay. We all awoke to the cacophonous sound of a pack of coyotes howling close by. Suddenly from under the bed, an ungodly howl arose. *Awwwooooooo wooooooo woooooo*. Rosebud was channeling her inner coyote. Those of us on top of the bed looked at each other, terror-stricken, our eyes huge, wondering if Rosebud had shape-shifted into a coyote underneath us. We braced ourselves as Rosie scrabbled out from under the bed frame. She looked scared that she might be *one of them*. She wasn't the only one. I slept with one eye open all night.

I'm wondering if the coyotes somehow sensed that I had recently written a chapter in this book about them. No coyote sightings had taken place here for nearly two years. Then I saw a huge one cross the road as I drove in my car. I knew it had to be an omen…and I was right. Two days after that sighting, Breezy had her very first coyote wrestling match. Years ago, both Shay and Rosebud had been attacked multiple times in my backyard, in broad daylight. Thus the need for baseball bats at every door, the better to smash in coyote craniums and save my pets. Breezy has lived here for over five years, and she had finally joined my other two dogs' coyote tussling histories.

Twenty degrees at dawn in late December. I didn't want to get up, but Rosebud insisted. I bundled up and went outside with her because I had a bad feeling about things. Rosie was done, so I brought her to the back door thinking she and I would go inside and I could burrow into the warm blankets a bit longer. Of course that's when Breezy decided *she* had to go, too.

Now two dogs were outside. Duke wisely decided to get more shut-eye and stayed in the house. I ignored my intuition and went back inside to feed the cats, leaving the girls outside. I heard Breezy bark which, to be perfectly honest, happens more than I would like and is in no way an unusual occurrence.

I glanced out the front windows but didn't see her. *Bark! Bark!* I turned to the window overlooking the side of the yard heading out to the pasture only to spot Breezy and a coyote up on their hind legs batting at each other, jaws snapping, biting at each other's forelegs and necks, going for the kill. They looked like two stallions in a dance to the death. Leaping, twirling, jaws snapping at each other's necks and forelegs. Breezy was holding her own. I give her credit for being such a badass, especially since both Shay and Rosebud had frozen in terror years ago when the coyotes tried to hamstring them before trying to rip out their throats. They hadn't fought back at all when the coyotes attacked them. Breezy, on the other hand, was giving as good as she got. Breezy is fierce when she needs to be. Kind of like me.

My body was moving before I fully comprehended what I was seeing and I was out the back door and into the porch. Looking out the porch windows, I saw them still fighting so I grabbed the baseball bat propped next to the outside door and ran out into the snow in my usual outfit of pajamas and slippers.

I stood for a moment, gathering my courage, took a deep breath, and charged forward, left arm out, fist clenched, and my right arm waving the bat above my head. Running toward them I roared at the top of my lungs. I didn't bother swearing this time, but kept roaring and running like Mel Gibson in the big battle scene in *Braveheart*. Usually in these situations I channel Xena, Warrior Princess, but this time I seemed to be impersonating Scottish warriors.

The coyote saw me and ran off a short distance, then stopped to watch me. I called for Breezy and my dog darted towards me, the fur raised on her back. The coyote turned to chase her. Breezy took that as a challenge and ran to meet it. I yelled for Breezy to come. Back and forth the coyote and Breezy went, fighting, chasing each other, and fighting some more. I stood in the snow, waving my baseball bat and roaring my battle cry. The coyote wasn't afraid of me in the least; although it did run off a few feet but then turned back once again to try to get at Breezy. I remember thinking, *Is this damn coyote ever going to give up?*

I finally got mad. I ran at that coyote, waving my club (err…my bat) like Ogg the Caveman attacking a Woolly Mammoth. I may have also picked up a few tips in warrior tactics from the hot Viking warriors in the TV series, *Vikings*. I absolutely love that show. This time, the coyote turned tail and ran into the horse pasture as I chased behind. I looked up the hill toward the mini mansion as I followed the coyote and noticed the big horses standing there, with hay in their mouths, watching the show. These horses gallop in terror when my dogs are in their pen. Why not when a real, live coyote is streaking along in their midst?

The stinking coyote stopped running, looked back over its shoulder, and turned to come at me. *Screw that,* I thought. *You don't own this place. I do.* I ran straight at it and didn't let up screaming except to order Breezy to get back to the house. The dog wanted to chase the coyote. The coyote wanted to eat the dog, and I was in the middle. I have been in this same situation far too many times.

I can't tell you how many times that damn animal ran off only to stop and look back over its shoulder at me before it ran off again, with me still in full pursuit. It was probably thinking, *What in God's name is WITH that woman? And will she PLEASE shut up!*

I continued to chase after it until it finally disappeared into the thick brush at the far end of the horse pasture. I leaned on the gate to catch my breath and waited to be sure the coyote didn't circle back. Then I remembered Rosebud had been outside the whole time. "Breezy! Where's Rosie? *Where is Rosie!?*"

She was safe on the steps by the front door. She's almost deaf so she may not have heard the ruckus, although it's hard to believe she hadn't heard me yelling. I'm sure people could have heard me in the next county.

Now I took Breezy to task. "That was a *coyote*. You don't ever fight coyotes. *Ever*. Get in the house! Now!" Up until then, Breezy was the only of my dogs that had not been attacked by coyotes. No longer. She has been officially inducted into the I've-been-bitten-by-a-mangy-coyote-and-lived-to-tell-about-it club.

All of this occurred at seven in the morning, and barely light outside. I hadn't had time for my coffee so all of this was highly annoying, to say the least. Ah yes, hobby farms. Highly overrated.

And wouldn't you know it—right before I wrote this chapter, I paused from making an egg salad sandwich and looked out the window only to witness a big coyote traversing my backyard at 2PM on a bright sunny day. Will this aggravation never end?

Breezy has always hated coyotes. Although she has now been in a fight with one she's not at all afraid of them, in fact, she goes looking for them. Faced with a coyote, Breezy's first instinct is to blast off after it and chase it off our property. I suppose it's part territorial, but more likely is she hates those animals with a passion and would kill them if she had a chance. Looking at her, you wouldn't think that she has the makings of a killer, but I've watched her chase after coyotes too many times with the single-minded intent of ending their sorry existence. I've only seen her fight the one coyote, but she has come home with bite wounds on her forelegs, so I have the sinking feeling she's gotten into a few rumbles out in the pasture on her own. Not the smartest thing to do, but she won't listen to me. Unfortunately, the Invisible Fence has long been broken, and the expense to fix it is out of my budget right now. So I have no way of keeping her in my yard, other than chaining her up, which I'd really rather not do.

It's one thing if Breezy were to fight only one coyote—she demonstrated she can hold her own—but if there is more than one, the odds of her surviving go down precipitously. Years ago, I'd watched a coyote lure my dog Rosebud and, while he had her attention, another coyote came out of nowhere behind her and latched onto her back leg. The first coyote was on her in a flash and the two of them were dragging her off towards the woods to kill her. She was too scared to fight back; she was frozen with terror. The same thing happened to Shay, twice. I was thankful that I witnessed the attacks because I was able to run off the coyotes by chasing after them.

On my way up to the chicken coop one day, I noticed a long, white bone sticking up out of the snow. I picked it up with my mittens and tried to figure out what it was, deciding that Breezy had somehow gotten her paws on a dead deer carcass and dragged part of it home. A few days later, some ribs showed up. Examining them closely, I knew they probably weren't from a deer. I watched Breezy that day, to learn where she had been finding her stash. Seeing her nonchalantly swagger back down the driveway from the direction of the road, I decided to do some sleuthing. She trotted alongside as I followed her paw prints in the snow, heading up the driveway. They didn't continue on out to the road, however, but veered off to the left and up a small hillock and into the woods fronting the road.

Peering down at her tracks, I continued on into the woods. Breezy was now off ahead of me somewhere. So many of her paw prints soon crisscrossed in the snow that I couldn't decide which to follow. I looked up to see her off in the woods, acting sneaky. Whenever she acts sneaky, that's when I know she's up to no good. Making my way over to where she had her snout dug down into the snow, I soon came upon what she had been dragging to our yard and feasting upon, and it wasn't a deer. It was a long-dead coyote. I knew it had been there for some time because all that was left were bones and the outer fur pelt. Its white skeleton was there in the snow Breezy had trampled on her many trips to the remains. The skull and most of the ribs were laid out in a clinical manner. The leg and arm bones were gone, consumed by Breezy and whoever else had happened upon it.

Breezy looked up at me guiltily, but also with excitement. She knew that I now knew she had been feasting upon her most hated nemesis—the wily coyote. She danced around the carcass, picking up

The coyote pelt—what's left of it, anyway

a bone and tossing it in the air with glee. *The only good coyote is a dead coyote*, I imagined her saying.

I shook my head and smiled, thankful her rabies and distemper shots were up-to-date, not knowing what had felled this coyote, whether disease or injury. We headed back down the driveway. She wanted to bring a bone with her, but I told her to leave it. I knew the minute I turned my back, she'd do it anyway. That's Breezy.

Days later on the trail to the coop, the entire spine was laying in the snow. I left it there and let Breezy have her fun. I knew I couldn't stop her. The spine soon disappeared, I assumed down her gullet. Eventually the coyote pelt was deposited in the yard in the same spot. I saw her gnawing with great satisfaction on it a number of times. Maybe she killed the damn thing, maybe not. But she certainly had her sweet revenge on her sworn enemy.

18

Day Tripping

One weekend day in late July, I had the novel idea to actually be social. This type of impulse is exceedingly rare for me—I prefer being alone and reading a really good book to being surrounded by masses of talking people. This may be the result of many years of working at the airport and being surrounded by angry, anxious, or disgruntled passengers, which seemed to be the three main flavors whenever I happened to be their gate agent. Plus I'm a confirmed and lifelong introvert.

On that summer day, however, I decided I could manage to be a social butterfly for an hour or two, and to go down to the local VFW to watch the annual Tractor Pull and perhaps quaff a beer or two. This would then qualify for my semi-annual going-out-and-having-a-couple jaunt, and I might actually enjoy myself.

Parking my car on the gravel road, I stepped out and began walking along the side of the road towards the festivities. The roar of souped-up lawn tractor engines was deafening, and I patted my pockets to be sure I'd remembered earplugs. For those of you who have never had the experience of seeing a tractor pull, I would explain its allure, but truly… there isn't any. The basic premise is a crowd full of men (and a few women) holding aloft their beers, standing behind a temporary fence, and watching one lawn tractor after another compete to drag a weight the farthest on a track in the dirt. I guess if you're a motorhead you can talk engines, and piston stroke, and compression, and all things of that ilk, while dreaming of having a muscle car with a 351 Cleveland, bored .30 over, with a glass pack, dual Holley carbs, and a racing cam. But I digress.

I can talk cars when I need to, work on my own cars if I have to, and drive my little red sports car like an Indy 500 driver any chance I get. Lawn tractors with V8 engines? That's *weird*. But as I said, I was attempting to be social, and so was willing to hang out and watch the dirt fly as tractor wheels dug in deeper in an attempt to eke out just one more foot to win the prize. I've never ascertained what exactly the prize is. A case of beer? A lifetime supply of chewing tobacco? Who knows? It probably doesn't matter to anyone, they simply want to get out there and play with their toys.

Musing on all of these things as I walked, I didn't notice the small dip in the road. I noticed soon enough for, when I put down my left foot in its bejeweled flip-flop, my ankle went one way, and my foot went the other. A loud *snap!* and I was down on my butt in the road, unable to get up. I knew I'd either broken or sprained my ankle. It turned out to be a combination of both. My car was hundreds of feet away and I knew I couldn't crawl that far on the hot gravel. I had fallen between two cars parked along the road. Luckily for me, a man was at that moment getting out of his car across the road from where I sat nursing my ankle. It hurt like mad already. He didn't see me, so I yelled for help. He got me up and helped me to the building where I found my neighbor, Jeff, who drove me back to my car on his four-wheeler and off to the urgent care I went.

I hopped all the way from my car in to the urgent care where, after X-rays, I was told my ankle was badly sprained and part of the bone had broken off. I had severely sprained the same ankle thirty years before and was expecting a plaster cast, but instead was fitted with a rigid plastic cast that could be removed via Velcro strips. It was ungainly and uncomfortable, but I didn't plan on taking that sucker off for a while. To complete my attire, I was given a pair of crutches and told to put no weight on the injured foot. Ugh. I tried to talk the doctor into giving me a walking cast, but he refused.

The tractor pull was still in full swing when I drove past on my way home from urgent care. I gave it barely a glance, gritting my teeth as I wondered how in the hell I was going to make it up all the steps to get into my house on crutches. And after that, how would I manage to feed the outside animals? Someone had to feed and water them. I knew I couldn't count on anyone else to do it twice a day for as long as it would take for my ankle to heal.

Depressed and in serious pain, I pulled up to the house and sat for a moment before opening the car door and maneuvering myself out, which wasn't easy, since it was my left leg that was injured. Holding onto the frame of the door, I lurched upright and wobbled on my right leg, trying my best to keep weight off my left foot. Next was hopping a few feet, grasping the car in a death grip all the while, in order to get the back door open where my crutches were nestled in the back seat. Having successfully accomplished this task, I placed the crutches under my arms and clumsily made my way over to the cement steps, where I took a moment to consider the best way to tackle the seemingly impossible ascent. I might as well have been scaling Mount Everest. I had barely set one crutch on the bottom step when I immediately face planted on the steps, skinning my right knee in the process. Luckily I hadn't broken my other leg in my fall although, considering how hard I hit, I'm surprised I didn't. In spite of that, the plastic cast held up admirably. I lay there for several minutes and shed a few tears, feeling horribly sorry for myself. Eventually I levered myself up and tackled the ascent again, this time scaling the mountain and making it to the front door, onward to the inside steps, and finally to the couch, where I lay in misery, contemplating the near future in all its dire entirety.

The dogs didn't care—they wanted to be fed, *immediately*, and the cats' food dish was empty, too. Great. And that was just a warm-up to what awaited me outside: two hungry mini horses, and two chicken coops filled with ravenous chickens. I'm thankful the llama and alpacas no longer lived here, and the goat and boarded horses hadn't yet moved in, so at least I didn't have to feed all of them. I didn't have to deal with the chickens until the next morning as they had already been fed that day. The mini horses were another matter. Hay twice a day, and water more often. How was I going to hold a piece of hay when both my hands had to be holding the crutches? And what about the water bucket?

Making my way down the steps to go outside was far easier than going up, as I simply sat my butt down on the topmost step and plopped my rear down, step by step. Once down all of the steps, I needed to hold onto something in order to get the crutches under me. I eventually made it to the driveway, and I turned to the garage to grab the hay. Don't ask me how I managed to keep hold of the hay while still learning how to walk with crutches, but I did. Twice a day, in fact.

The water bucket presented a bigger problem. The only outside spigot was way around the rear of the house. Necessity, as they say, is the mother of invention. I grabbed the small bucket I usually used, as well as a five-gallon bucket and cover and put them in the car trunk, then drove the car up the hill and around the side of my house and over to the spigot, backing the car as close to it as I could get. Hefting myself and crutches out of the car, I grabbed the small bucket—which barely fit under the spigot—and bent over the faucet. I did my best not to topple over as I filled it, and then hopped with it, crutchless, over to the trunk, sloshing water all the way. Upending the contents into the five-gallon bucket, I did this again and again, until the larger bucket was full. I then secured the cover on it as I didn't want to deal with five gallons of water sloshing around in my trunk if it fell over on the drive back down the hill to the minis' garage.

The biggest problem was in getting that heavy five-gallon bucket out of the trunk. I couldn't do it with the crutches in the way, so instead I held the bucket and hopped on my right leg over to their water container. It sucked, big time, but I had no choice. Who did I know that would be willing to come over twice a day to help me? No one. They all worked, and had lives of their own, so I resolved to myself that I would figure it out, once again, alone. There are definitely times this gets to be too much for me, but I'm all about rising up and tackling the challenges, even when I've been beaten down repeatedly.

The next day was another lesson in resilience. Not only did I have to repeat the mini horse routine, I also had to make my way to two coops. The Coop de Ville is located at the far edge of the yard, near the pasture, so it's somewhat of a slog to go up there. I solved the problem by driving my car over there after filling the five-gallon bucket. Now I could feed and water them in the same trip. It wasn't much fun trying to use crutches inside the coop while attempting not to get any chicken manure on the bottoms, since I also had to use the crutches in my house, not to mention trying not to fall over the hungry, milling horde of chickens.

Once this monumental feat was accomplished, it was off to the Hillbilly Hotel where four roosters and five hens were still living. They were bound to be hungry, like usual, and I knew they would lay in wait to trip me. This coop was a more difficult endeavor. Due to the haphazard "construction" of the chicken run, I had to pull open a section of chicken wire secured by a bungee cord to the other side, move all of this out of my and my crutches' way, and then duck underneath the overhanging bird netting, all while holding a bucket of water and crutches. Then it was back out to grab the bucket of chicken chow, and repeat the entire process, all the while sweating like crazy in the heat.

Putting those chickens to bed at night was an absolute nightmare.

The big hens were far better behaved in this aspect, even in light of their bullying tendencies. I could count on them to already have hopped up and into the coop before dusk. Reggie and Aldrich were fine, too. The others—Nigel, Alfred, Lola, and Bianca—who had been recently relocated from the minis' garage, were like toddlers who refuse to go to bed. Can you imagine what it was like chasing four tiny, preternaturally fast chickens in a ten-foot by ten-foot area, dodging bird netting and food and water dishes, while maneuvering with crutches? The little bastards were like velociraptors. I really should have let the little jerks stay out and face the consequences when the Raccoon Family of Five made their nightly rounds. Who knows why I didn't—they pissed me off enough.

A week after my injury, I had an appointment with the orthopedic specialist, who wanted to fit me for a "boot." I asked him what that looked like, and once informed, told him no way was that going to work, because I had to walk in chicken and horse poop every day. Was there any other option? I pushed for the walking cast again, because I knew what that was like from thirty years ago, and I knew I could make it work. The crutches, however, definitely had to go. Once the doctor heard about the manure issue, he conferred, with somewhat raised eyebrows, with his nurse. They decided to take pity on me and I was outfitted with a rigid ankle brace. It was a series of interweaving pieces of fabric, all held together by industrial strength velcro. Although the doctor told me to keep off my foot and continue to use the crutches while only gradually putting more weight on my foot, by the time I got home I tossed those damn crutches aside and just went for it. I hopped a bit on my injured foot at first, but I was able, with the new brace, to actually walk again, and wear shoes. The ankle brace was like a *miracle*. I'd like to nominate whoever invented it for a Nobel Prize. Seriously, my life could begin anew—I no longer had to drive my car all over the yard and smash the weeds and what little grass existed into a pulp while making tire ruts everywhere the eye could see. No, I could *walk*. You have no idea how important something like that is until you can't do it anymore. My life was now simpler. Well, that's pushing things, isn't it? Okay, perhaps a bit simpler. Life goes on. The critters still have to be fed. Manure still has to be slung. And so it goes, day after day.

19

A Wheelie Good Thing

My cat Hissy was now seventeen-and-a-half years old, diabetic, with numerous health problems. I knew it was only a matter of time before I lost him, but I was determined to make sure his last days were comfortable. Eventually his back legs had become weak, to the point he could only walk a few steps, legs dragging behind him, before needing to lay down and rest. I kept asking him if he wanted to have me take him to the vet, but I got the strong feeling he wanted to die at home. Although his health was so fragile, he somehow still religiously used the litter box, unlike one of the younger and perfectly healthy cats, whose name shall go unmentioned.

To help him maneuver around the house, I decided to make him a wheelchair, since his front legs were working just fine. I'd seen photos of dogs in wheelchairs, so why not a cat? Researching "dog wheelchairs" on the internet, I looked at a ton of photos, and drew a schematic of what I thought would work. I measured Hissy, trying to hold him upright as I held out a tape measure, and jotted down measurements. I figured I could use a cat harness I already had (actually a rabbit harness, but the people at the feed store told me it could also be used with cats), PVC pipe for the wheelchair itself, two small tires of some type for mobility, and a foam pad over the PVC for Hissy's hips to rest on.

Armed with my scribbled notes, I drove to the hardware store in town. I wandered the aisles, trying to figure out what would work the best, glancing at my drawings, and scratching my head a bit in confusion. It's not like I'm a mechanical engineer or a rocket scientist—designing a prototype is hard for me to figure out. Clutching my hand-drawn plans, I snatched up first this implement, then that, comparing it to the drawing, and putting it back on the shelf. PVC pipe, wheels, bolts, nuts, washers—my mind was spinning.

An employee saw me wandering around in the PVC pipe aisle, holding an L-shaped connector, and took pity on me. I breathed a sigh of relief and held out my hand-drawn picture, and stammered, "Well… you're going to think I'm a little weird…I'm trying to build this." I handed him the drawing.

"No, it's okay. We get a lot of weird stuff in here," he said as he took it and turned it this way and that, finally settling on what looked to him as the correct orientation.

I grabbed it out of his hands. "No—you have it upside down." I turned it the right way and gave it back to him.

I explained the items on my list; this length, that angle, etc. Picking up a short angled piece of PVC he asked, "Does this look like what you need?" and handed it to me.

"Umm…yeah, I think so…" as I turned it over in my hands. As we narrowed our choice of materials, all the while referring to my world-class engineering blueprint, he turned to me and asked, "So, what are we building anyway?"

"I'm building my cat a wheelchair," I said in a conspiratorial whisper as I looked around furtively to see who else might be near enough to hear.

Dead silence. He took the PVC section from me and set it back on the shelf. "A *what?*"

"Wheelchair. He's really old and sick and he's having trouble with his back legs, " I said while discreetly glancing at him out of the side of my eye while I reached out to grab another connector piece.

He was motionless, staring at me with his mouth slightly agape. That's when I noticed his name tag. It said "Assistant Manager." Great. He wasn't just a lowly clerk. I had to get the almost-head honcho. It wasn't my luck to be dealing with a flunky who would soon be off to another job and I'd never see him again. No. This guy was more than likely to stay and I'd need to relive this humiliation over and over each time I had need of items from the hardware store.

Cringing a bit, I decided, *What the hell,* and faced him head on, letting him get a good look at me so he could identify me in the future and run off in another direction to avoid me. I acted like what I was there for was typical of any other Joe Blow who came in to shop.

Having clearly come to the unmistakable (and probably warranted) conclusion that I was several bricks short of a full load, he looked down at my drawing and said rather too brightly, "Oh! So *that's* what this is."

"I'm sure you've never had anyone come in with exactly this particular thing, have you?" I said, hoping I was exuding the proper and socially accepted amounts of normalness and sanity.

Silence again for a few beats too long and then his reply came, "Oh," he said, struggling to find the words, "People come in here with…engineering problems…all the time." I'm sure as he said this he was glad we were in the PVC pipe aisle rather than, say, the *knife* aisle. You never know what a lunatic-cat-wheelchair-person might be capable of.

Satisfied I was the only person who had ever darkened his door with *this* particular "engineering problem," I smirked a little inside and turned back to the array of PVC doodads. "Ok, what else do we need?"

I could tell he came to an internal decision after wrestling with himself as to whether I was crazy or not. Odd, yes. Loony? He must have decided not, because he then gave it his all and even seemed rather enthusiastic about solving the problem at hand—the wheelchair... not me. I think. Or perhaps he wanted to hurry up and find everything I needed so he could get rid of me and go tell everyone else in the store about his crazy customer. It happens.

When we got to the wheels, we both decided, given what he had in stock on the shelf, that it wasn't going to work. An image flashed into my mind and I blurted, "Tennis balls! We need tennis balls!"

Note how I said "we" rather than the singular "I." Like it or not, he was in this with me—lock, stock, and barrel. He was now part of my mad plan to construct a wheelchair for my cat.

He faltered for a moment and I thought I might have finally pushed him too far. "Why do you want tennis balls?"

"Old people put them on the bottom of their walkers so they slide easily on floors." *See,* my eyes gleamed with triumph as I beamed the thought wave to him, *I'm not* completely *nuts. There is a method to my madness!*

Happily carrying all of my purchases to the cashier, I left him behind in aisle eight.

Once home, I sat down on the floor and laid out the wheelchair supplies. I needed two pieces of nine-inch PVC pipe for the sides. Two more pieces for the back axle, but this time six inches long. Two 90-degree pieces to connect the long sides to the back and back upright pieces. The back axle would connect between T-shaped pieces on the rear upright pipes. The tennis balls would go on the front and back bottoms to allow Hissy to slide on the wood floor.

I went downstairs and dug out a hacksaw to cut the pieces to size and then hauled Hissy over from his comfy cat bed to do a final measurement. He purred along as I sawed through the plastic. Inserting the various pieces together, I held it up under him, set him back down, and grabbed the hacksaw to adjust the length of the front to be lower as his legs were hanging in midair the way I had cut it. Once it was done,

I glued all the pieces together and let them harden up. Then I added the piece of foam (the foam insulation that goes over water pipes worked perfectly) around the back crosspiece where his back end would drape over, with his hind legs behind all of it. The tennis balls were the hardest part. In order to get them onto the bottom of the pipes, I had to cut an X into them. None of my knives are remotely sharp, and I went in search of a box cutter. I then had to be sure I didn't cut off any fingers while trying to cut the X into the tennis balls while they tried to roll around under my hand. After much sweating and swearing, they finally cooperated, and I placed them on the pipes.

Once the PVC cement was dry, out came the cat harness and I strapped Hissy into it. I had drilled holes through the horizontal pieces and threaded a thin rope through and tied it around the pipes, and then connected that to the harness. Standing him up inside the contraption, I realized the cat harness wasn't going to work. It wouldn't support him enough so that he could "walk." He hung suspended in midair with his legs dangling and it didn't look like much fun.

Rummaging around the house, I found an old pair of nylons in a drawer in the spare bedroom. I had sworn off the revolting things years

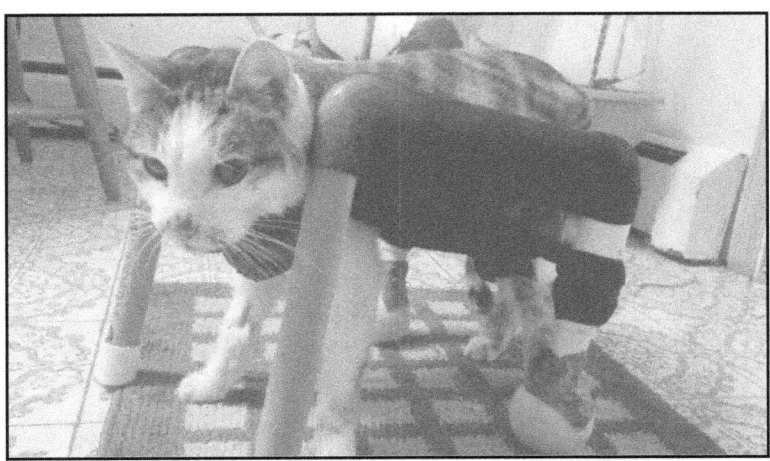

Hissy testing out his under-construction wheelchair

ago as they made me feel like a sausage in its casing. I brought them to the wheelchair and figured out how to drape and tie them around the PVC so that they made a sling where Hissy's entire body, other than his legs, could comfortably rest atop. Picking him up again from another nice nap in his comfy bed, I placed him on top of the nylon sling and watched as he used his front legs to drag himself slowly across the floor, purring all the way. Hissy was able to use his wheelchair for only a short time, until he became too weak. And then the sad day came all too soon, and he went on his journey to the other side to join his late brother Stripey and all of his other cat, dog, and even a few chicken friends. I really miss him.

He was such a sweet guy. Though his time on Earth was drawing to a close, I know he appreciated my efforts.

20

A Horse Is A Horse, Of Course, Of Course...

It was the first time I had taken Misty, the mini horse, and Duke, the dog, for a walk together on the road. I had no idea how the two of them would be together on a walk. Duke is an incredibly calm and patient dog—until he's hungry, and then all bets are off. Misty, on the other hand, can be headstrong and impetuous. She likes to have her way. After haltering her, we set off up the driveway, Duke on a leash to my left, and Misty on my right. Duke seemed to really like going on a walk with a mini horse, but Misty wasn't as sure that being seen palling around with a dog was up to snuff. Horses are rather snobbish that way, minis especially.

We reached the end of my long driveway and took a left, walking down the gravel road towards the dead end. The land to our right was all part of the regional park, and tons of people hike and jog along the miles of trails.

People walking along the nearest park trail could see the three of us out on the road and gave us second and third looks, trying to figure out what they were seeing. Misty isn't much taller than Duke, and is light-colored like him, so at first glance, she may have looked like a dog. Being the observant and proud miniature horse she is, Misty noticed the people watching her and, to make sure they knew she was a *horse* and not a lowly *dog,* she whinnied loudly and trotted a bit with her head held high. The people broke out into huge smiles and waved at us.

Another day the three of us set out to walk the trails in the park. On one of the maintenance roads, a worker riding a tractor saw us and waved with a big smile as he drove by. Duke was tiring, so I brought him and Misty home and then haltered up Sunny and took her for a solo walk down the road. Later, another park worker drove by us in his work truck, then turned around, and stopped to talk to me. He said he'd had draft horses when he was growing up, so we talked about horses for a while. He had just dropped off his coworker at the park maintenance facility and the other guy had asked him to drive back to the road and see what exactly the two of them had just seen on the road—meaning me with my mini horse and a dog.

The coworker had said to him when they drove along and saw Sunny in the distance, "Is that a dog? It looks like a dog."

"No, dude, that's a horse," the guy (who was in his work truck now talking to me) had replied to his coworker.

"No way, man, that's *got* to be a dog!" the coworker said. My guy had been right that it was a horse, but had to drive back to double-check and see for himself.

Just wait until the park workers see me walking down the road with a dog and Donald the incredible wonder goat!

21

Dog Days

It was one of those truly delightful early April days in Minnesota, with a cold, grey sky and sleet hammering down. Just when you think it might actually be spring, and then the weather gods say, *Uh uh, we aren't done with you yet.*

Breezy and Rosie were on house arrest, relegated to being hooked up to tie-outs on the front steps and lawn, since they had recently gone on their extended excursion to the four-lane highway several miles from my house. Not wanting to sit out there with them and freeze my own butt off, I was inside the house, working on my laptop at the dining room table.

Bark! Bark! Venturing out to the porch, I looked towards the woods at the object of Breezy's attention. A lone deer stood there. It tentatively came closer, up to the edge of the lawn, and delicately stamped its right foot several times. It nibbled on bark and twigs, considering whether to cross the yard past the dogs, eventually deciding against it, and slowly it meandered back up the trail into the deeper woods.

It had to totally kill Breezy that she couldn't chase after it, and she sat despondently at the end of her leash. I didn't have much sympathy for her, not after that last escapade, and I sat down at my computer and went back to work. Not twenty minutes later, once again I heard, *Bark! Bark! Bark!* This time I had to go to the front window to see what the big deal was. A male mallard duck was toddling along in the front yard. Poor Breezy. So close and yet so unattainable as she strained at the limits of her tie-out. It's almost like the local prey animals were coming to thumb their noses at her. Good for them.

Later that year on Thanksgiving day, the first snowfall of the winter fell; barely an inch of white stuff. I was in the garage, cleaning and moving stuff to make room for my car when winter finally hit in full force. I kept hearing a weird noise but didn't realize the source of it until I looked out into the front yard to see that Rosie had fallen through the ice in the front garden pond. It's a three-foot-deep, eight-foot wide circular pond with smooth sides. She's had Lyme disease and is arthritic, plus can't bark anymore because of a tumor on her jaw that can't be removed. Only her head was above water and she was too weak to pull herself out. I dropped the broom, ran out there, and dragged her to safety by her front legs. She had gone to get a drink from the pond as she likes doing in the summer. The pond had iced over in the cold weather, but it wasn't yet thick enough to hold her weight, and in she went.

Duke is a year younger than Rosie, but if anything, his arthritis is worse than hers. He's a big dog, part Husky and supposedly part Arctic Wolf, and he weighs over a hundred pounds. He too fell into the garden pond, a month before Rosie did. He was tall enough that he could have gotten himself out, but wasn't strong enough because of the arthritis in his lower back and hips. He barked for me to come rescue him. Come to think of it, he barks for me to do *everything* for him. He can be rather demanding at times. I really don't know how I pulled him out of there without falling in myself, but I did. It wasn't easy. After he was safely back on dry ground, he seemed to think it was funny that he had fallen in. At least that was the expression on his furry face as he looked back over his shoulder at the pond. He didn't seem to be any worse for wear, so I walked him back to the house and towelled him off.

Late December and seven inches of new, light, fluffy snow had fallen. So fluffy, in fact, it was hard to walk in it to feed the outside animals, and I worried I'd turn my ankle and sprain it again like I'd done the previous summer. I pictured myself stranded out there, crawling through the snow for days trying to get back to the house. Whenever I put my boot down, my leg would slide off to the side. Same thing with the other foot, but it slid a different direction. Great for toning my thigh muscles, but tiring nonetheless. I am not much for strenuous exercise. A comfy chair, a good book, and a mug of hot tea are my version of exercise. It takes a lot of energy to turn the pages, particularly with a cat curled up on top of the open book in my lap. And lifting the mug on top of all that? *Exhausting.*

A while later, the dogs were outside. Only two days before, Breezy and the coyote had been in their knock-down, drag-out boxing match. I thought I heard the sound of coyotes yipping, so I opened the door to bring in the dogs. Only Rosie was there. I ran outside along the sidewalk to look out at the horse pasture, calling for Breezy and Duke, clad as usual in my jammies and wearing Crocs. Nothing. No sight of them. Back in the house, I threw on my boots and parka, muttering, "Why don't they *ever* listen? *Why?* I am *sooo* tired of this stuff happening!" I made my way up to the pole barn, struggling through the snow. Breezy appeared, running like a bat out of hell from the back forty with her tail between her legs and looking behind her as she ran. Duke was nowhere in sight.

"Breezy! Where is Duke?" I yelled.

I ducked between the horse fence wires. One of the big horses followed me as I stalked through their paddock towards the back fence line, where I went between the wires and waved for Breezy to come help me look for Duke. Stumbling and sliding, I used the end of my baseball bat (you didn't think for a second I wouldn't bring *that* with me, did you? I'm no dummy) as a walking stick. I made my way down an incline and from there slogged up the big hill in the back, trying to follow the trail the horses had laid down in the snow, thinking it would be easier to walk. Ha. It wasn't.

I was now in full view of the McMansion on the top of the hill, its huge bank of windows looking accusingly down on me. They'd had a prime view in the past of my various critter-related misadventures, and I cringed, hoping no one was home to watch me struggling to walk in the snow. I can only imagine what they would think I was doing. A woman in the dead of winter, in her pajamas and parka, holding a baseball bat, and wandering in circles out in the middle of the pasture accompanied by a dog, yelling for something no one could see. No wonder they soon put their house up for sale and moved. I would too.

Breezy leaped like a deer through the snow ahead of me. Fearing the worst, I scanned the snow, but didn't see a lump of cream-colored dog fur anywhere. I spun around in a circle (I hope they weren't watching me then) shading my eyes to see in the glare off the blinding white

Rosebud slogging through twelve inches of fresh snow

snow. No Duke. What was I going to tell his dad? My heart pounding from the exertion, I made my way back through the snow to the house. Have you ever noticed that "snow" is a four-letter word? There's a reason for that. No Duke by the front steps. Rosie had run up to the pole barn while Breezy and I were out in the pasture and refused to come to the house when I called. She was worried the coyotes would get her, not to mention she was nearly deaf and probably couldn't hear me calling for her.

I was completely spent. No way could I make the slog back up to the pole barn to get her. I lay down on my back in the snow, panting in exhaustion, mindlessly repeating, *"Why?"* over and over. Breezy came over to lick my face; perhaps she thought that was the equivalent of doggie CPR. I was able to get her to bark loudly by exclaiming, "Where's Rosie? Go find Rosie!" It worked. Rosie heard her barking and came running and we all went inside.

And where was Duke this whole time? I'd somehow completely forgotten he was *inside the house* and sacked out, sleeping, in the living room the entire time. Coyote-induced stress will do that to you. My high-intensity cardio workout in the back forty was in vain. A fool's errand.

22

SIMPLY NUTS

Squirrels. I've heard them referred to as "tree rats." I don't mind the grey squirrels, even when they eat all the bird feed, but red squirrels are my nemesis. Barely half the size of the grey version, red squirrels are bossy, argumentative, scrappy, and highly destructive to house and home. They tend to be nasty little suckers, chasing the much larger grey squirrels mercilessly across the yard in territorial disputes over the bird food. I remember coming home from elementary school one afternoon, and my dad finding a red squirrel tail out in the backyard near the bird feeder. Only the tail was there; the rest of the squirrel was missing in action. Upon questioning, my ostensibly gentle mother, who wouldn't hurt a fly, admitted she had opened the back window, leaned out with a .22 rifle, and blown that little bastard to kingdom come. That's how much she hated them.

It took me longer to come to the same state of mind, but now I too don't like the scrawny little creeps. At first they contented themselves with chewing the soffit on the minis' garage, gnawing huge holes in the wood with their sharp little teeth, thereby gaining egress to the rafters of the garage where they set up a cozy nest of oak leaves and assorted other items. I hired a wildlife removal expert to, well, *remove them*, and figured that was that. Oh no, that was definitely *not* that, and the squirrels soon upped the ante and gnawed through the two-by-fours covering the edge of my house's roof, gaining entry to the palatial expanses of my attic, and all the cushy, comfy insulation they could toss into the air as they burrowed down with glee.

Sitting in the living room one winter evening, I heard the most distressing noise: the sound of gnawing little rodent teeth sawing through the two by fours in one of the walls. Deciding it wasn't actually a poltergeist coming after me, but was in reality some type of rodent, I walked over to the wall and pounded on it repeatedly, while yelling, "Knock it the hell off!"

Several days later I was out in the yard and heard the scurrying of tiny feet on the roof shingles. A small, furry red head popped over the edge and looked down on at me, and that's when I knew who the chewing culprit was—a red squirrel. I raised my fist at it and said, "You had better move your butt out of that attic right now, or face the consequences!"

Of course the deviant creature paid me no mind, and taunted me with its presence whenever I was outside, making sure I knew it was there by chittering loudly at me. I called my brother and asked him what I could do about the squirrel infestation in my attic. He came over and placed some rat traps laden with peanut butter on the roof near their entrance. I happily contemplated soon having a squirrel-free existence. It was not to be.

Walking around the side of the house on a sunny afternoon, my attention was yanked upward by the noise of a red squirrel in full rant. It stood upright on its hind legs near the peak of the roof, directly in front of the rat traps and glared down at me, swearing a blue streak in squirrel language, obviously angry as hell I had dared to attempt to murder it. Looking up at it, I grew tired of being yelled at. "Yeah?

Do you think I care? You're chewing my house up. You need to move out or *you are going to die.*"

Wriggling its whiskers and probably also giving me the finger, it then turned its back on me and ran off across the roof, leaped onto the branch of an overhanging black walnut tree, scampered down the trunk, and took off across the lawn. Unfortunately, that wasn't the last I saw of it, not to mention its ever-expanding family

A few mornings later, one launched itself bodily at the dining room window as I sat inside, its claws scratching at the glass. She perched on a branch in the tree by the house, chittering angrily, then jumped onto the roof and ran about wildly. I could hear her tiny feet pounding across the roof, back and forth, back and forth. Breezy was going nuts in the house, barking and running around trying to find it. Soon after, I was in the living room and noticed the squirrel sitting on another tree limb, watching me like the evil doll in the movie *Chuckie*. I refused to be bullied, and said to her, "I told you not to live in my attic. I warned you," as she continued to stare daggers at me. I swear she had her hands on her hips as she glared at me, angered by my attempt to exterminate her entire family.

It started out with a mama squirrel and two cute babies taking up residence in my attic. Now I'm sure far more exist. They are rather like cockroaches—if you see one, that means 8,000 more are in hiding. I'm still fighting to remove them from my house.

Back when I didn't actively plot their deaths, I found a baby red

Nutter keeping an eye on a grey squirrel tormenting him from the outside hanging basket

squirrel hiding in the wheel well of my Jeep. I forgot all about him, and a while later hopped in and started it up. He must have made his way under the hood into the engine compartment and onto the fan belt in my absence because I soon saw him flung out and onto the ground. He sat stunned in the snow for at least ten minutes while I warmed up the Jeep with the heater blasting. I hopped out and asked him if he was okay, as he was a cute little thing. I knew nothing at that point about their latent evil tendencies.

Several days later I opened the back porch door to let out the dogs, and he, or another of his ilk, nearly darted inside while I stood at the open door. I screamed, he scrambled off, and the dogs were in mad pursuit. He ran hell-bent for leather to the nearest tree and made it out alive.

Another day, another squirrel drama: I couldn't figure out what were the repeated loud *thunks!* I'd been hearing somewhere in the yard, until I looked up and saw a red squirrel high in the black walnut tree, pulling the green walnuts off the branches and hurling them down to the ground for later retrieval and hoarding for winter. The walnut makes a singular type of sound as it crashes through the leaf canopy and branches, tumbling from far above until it hits the ground and bounces a few times.

Breezy and I walked toward the tree and I thought, *Well, if they're falling, I may as well harvest them.* Suddenly the walnuts rained down like hail. I looked up at the squirrel as it halted in mid-scamper on a tree branch thirty feet up. "So you're the one making all this noise!" It flicked its tail as I spoke, wringing its front paws together. "What if I take some of these walnuts you've thrown to the ground?" I asked. It glared down at me as if to say, *You'd better not!* And it returned to dropping walnuts.

This type of walnut comes encased in a round, bright green shell, with the walnut meat nestled inside an inner indestructible casing—it looks rather like a small cannonball, and I imagine it would feel pretty much like being shot by one had one of those green scud missiles ever hit me head on. I had to remind myself every time I walked to the chicken coop to steer far clear of the walnut tree so I wouldn't be thwacked on the head by a 100 mph black walnut. Being hit by one of those bad boys would almost certainly have rendered me unconscious, left me with a huge lump on my head once I finally awoke, and sprawled out on the lawn with cackling, victorious red squirrels doing high-fives far above me in the tree.

It was early fall, and the black walnuts were fully ripe and ready to be turned into airborne missiles by homicidal squirrels. I set up a patio umbrella above the hammock to ensure all parts of me were safely curled up underneath. Breezy hopped onto the hammock next to me, and we nestled under a blanket to read a book and then, hopefully, enjoy a well-deserved nap. Grey squirrels scampered about through the fallen leaves nearby, gathering walnuts the red squirrels had launched to the ground. I sighed with contentment and snuggled down deeper to nap. These squirrels were soon chased off by a gang of tiny red squirrels, who had realized the grey guys were stealing their hard-won bounty. Breezy watched the takedown through sleepy, half-open eyes.

One of the grey squirrels dropped his walnut and ran for the hills, chased by a pack of reds. A red squirrel acting as lookout stood on the roof of the house fifteen feet away from me. Another perched on a branch above and to my right. Both were chittering angrily at top volume, complaining about the grey thieves. Unable to sleep due to the unrelenting clamor, I opened one eye and saw a red squirrel staring down at me from the tree, "What are *you* looking at?" I asked.

It grabbed a walnut, ran across the branch, leaped to the roof and darted through the hole it had chewed into my attic. Wonderful. It wasn't only a nest of squirrels in my attic, but also their huge cache of black walnuts. The furry rodent popped back out and came to the eave of the roof, looking down its nose at me. "You're gonna die, sucker, if you don't move out of my house!" I threatened.

Suddenly squirrels were swirling up and down the nearby tree trunk, while red and grey squirrels were duking it out under me. A grey took off, and a red hovered on the side of the trunk, not ten feet from where we lay on the hammock. It ran up the tree and began to launch walnuts with pinpoint accuracy from forty feet up. The damn thing calculated trajectory and terminal velocity of each walnut, while allowing for variances in wind speed and direction. It was launching walnuts with precision, with an eye to achieving maximum collateral damage and destructive mayhem.

I pulled my legs up, curled myself into a fetal position and prayed my frayed old patio umbrella could withstand the barrage of missiles. Now I understood the source of the huge hole in the plastic table where my book rested—an incoming walnut at warp speed. That could have been my *head*. I have been accused in the past of having a hole in my head, but this shit was real...I was under full-scale aerial bombardment!

Grey squirrels are not as fast as the reds. In an Olympic sprinting competition, red squirrels would win every time. With a walnut clutched in its jaws, a grey ran madly across the yard, making for the safety of the woods. The pursuing red accelerated like a sports car on nitro and gained on the grey, finally body-slamming into it. They tumbled end over end. The grey lost its grip on the walnut and ran for its life. The little red squirrel snatched up its prize and stood up on its hind legs to claim utter squirrel dominance. All it needed was the theme from *Rocky* to make its victory dance complete. It ran back up the walnut tree next to the hammock Breezy and I were under and resumed launching walnut missiles to the ground. I'm not sure how Breezy managed to keep herself from leaping from the hammock to chase the squirrels after all this excitement. The sheer number of the foul, furry creatures must have overloaded her circuits and she decided to just skip it.

23

Chicken-Hearted

Furelli was a white Silkie hen, and was Filbert and Phoebe's firstborn. She was my absolute favorite chicken ever, other than Filbert and Ursula. She had the sweetest personality, and was unbelievably cute. When she was barely six months old, she attempted to lay her first egg. As sometimes happens with hens and their first eggs, she became egg bound, meaning the egg wasn't fully expelled from her body. Not only was she egg bound, but she had also prolapsed, and part of her insides were now *outside* her body.

When I found her after work one night, she was on her side, with blood all over her rear end. I lifted her to see what was going on, and that's when I saw the egg protruding a third of the way out, with bloody tissue tightly adhering to it. She must have been there for a while and was close to dying. I did my best to clean her up with a wet paper towel, but I couldn't do a thing about getting the egg loose without killing her.

I had previously taken another hen to the animal emergency room, so off we went. By the time we got there, it was after eleven at night and it took a while before we were ushered into a room. The vet examined

Furelli's baby photo

her and then brought her into another part of the animal hospital. I sat alone in the room waiting, idly paging through fashion magazines and not seeing a bit of them, too worried about Furelli to focus on much of anything.

When the vet returned to the room, his expression didn't bode well. He explained she was egg bound and had prolapsed, which I already knew, and suggested the best thing to do was to put her down so she didn't suffer. He believed that, if she did pull through, the next egg she laid would probably kill her, since her oviduct (where the egg travels through before it's laid) would never be normal, any future eggs would become stuck deep inside her, and she would suffer peritonitis and die a very painful death.

I'm highly resourceful when it comes to caring for animals, so I didn't fully believe this was Furelli's death sentence. I asked the vet to remove the stuck egg and do the best he could to get her insides back inside her, and then stitch her up. I would take her home and see what I could do. He walked out of the room shaking his head, but he did as I asked. Several hundred dollars and several hours later, I walked out with Furelli and a bottle of antibiotics meant to forestall an internal infection.

Furelli took up residence in a box in the house where I did my best to make her comfortable. Trying to give liquid antibiotics to a chicken is not my favorite way to spend my time, but I did it. You have to be very careful not to squirt the liquid the wrong way in their beak, as they can easily aspirate it into their air sacs and that would be all she wrote—

the chicken would most likely die as a result. Previously I had endured the sheer delight of giving liquid medicine to a pair of cockatiels I had owned; a chicken was much easier to manage.

I called around the metro area to find a vet who specialized in chickens and ended up bringing her to one for follow-up visits, and to remove the stitches on her butt. Concerned about her laying another egg, I asked the vet what could be done. Believe it or not, they can give some kind of shot to birds which works to inhibit the hormones that cause ovulation. Kind of like "the Pill" for birds, it needs to be given regularly, or ovulation occurs and a day or so later out comes an egg.

This soon became too expensive, even for me, the profligate spender on all things animal. I decided to research any herbal or holistic remedies that might work, and learned a homeopathic remedy, Sepia, will stop chickens from laying eggs. There were also other remedies to help with thin-shelled eggs, and all manner of other chicken maladies. I zoomed over to the health food store and stocked up. Trying to figure out how I would get Furelli to ingest the remedies was the next dilemma. I solved the problem two ways. These remedies come in the form of tiny round balls, so I put a few of them in a small plastic container, filled it with water, and let them melt. Once they had gone into solution, I grabbed a small plastic syringe (no needle attached) I had in my possession from giving injections to the alpacas, and sucked up some of the solution into the syringe. Then it was simply a matter of carefully squirting a tiny amount into Furellis' beak and *Voila!* no eggs. The other way was to make a small bowl of chicken oatmeal (basically moistened chicken chow) and then sprinkle a couple of the round balls on top. Furelli always snapped up the balls first.

Eventually I slacked off on giving her the medicine, until one day I saw an egg laying on the ground. So much for that vet's opinion—she had successfully laid an egg, it hadn't gotten stuck, and she hadn't died. Imagine that—he had gone to how many years of school to become

Furelli floating in the tub

educated, while I relied on my skills in research along with my gut feeling about what to do. Not that I consider myself anywhere near his equal in animal-related matters, but I was proud of proving him wrong.

Over the following years, Furelli laid many more eggs, and experienced egg binding only a couple of times. She never prolapsed again. I now knew what to look for, and could tell when she was having problems laying an egg. Again I figured out how to solve the problem—I found a plastic tub in the basement and filled it up halfway with warm water. Then I put Furelli in the tub, where she floated around, her feet touching the bottom. She usually fell asleep in the tub; she was a lot like me that way. The warm water relaxed her muscles enough that the egg dropped right out and I'd find it on the bottom of the plastic tub. Removing her from the water, I towel dried her and then used the blow dryer, set on low, to finish her spa treatment. She actually loved getting blow dried. She was a funny little chicken. She probably would have let me paint her nails, too. No, I did *not* try it, but considering how adorable she was, I think a nice hot-pink nail polish would have gone well with her fluffy white feathers.

Filbert was my first rooster, and was the progenitor of every other chick hatched here. He was a great-grandfather many times over. A black Silkie with a crossed-beak, he came to live here as a young chicken, along with Phoebe and Celeste, two white Silkie hens. He lived to the ripe old age of nine years, which is ancient in chicken years. Phoebe preceded him in death a year prior, but Celeste is still going strong at nearly twelve years old.

The first chick he fathered was Furelli, and after that I lost count of who did what to whom. Chickens are like rabbits that way.

He was a wonderful rooster, and very protective of his flock. As each successive wave of chicks hatched, the odds favored half of them to be roosters, and so it was. Filbert carefully watched over each chick. As these new roosters matured, eventually they all tried to topple Filbert from his perch as top rooster in the coop. I had to find new homes for several of them over the years because they probably would have killed each other. I never considered giving Filbert away, though. He was my favorite rooster out of all of them, and there have been over a dozen roosters over the years.

For the most part he was calm but sometimes, when I was out in the coop cleaning, he would take exception to whatever I was doing and fly off the handle in frustration or anger. When he was young, I remember him leaping up at me, and twirling in the air at me, spurs extended. He was small enough that it wouldn't have hurt much had he connected, but I couldn't let him think he could bully me. As he leaped into the air and lashed out, I reached out and snatched him from midair like a thrown football. I started to call him "my little football." I don't know whether he liked the name. I did, especially in later years when he mellowed and I carried him around like a little football, nestled in my arms. He cooed with contentment whenever I carried him.

He could also be affectionate, and would hop up into my lap and mutter sweet nothings to me when his other girls weren't looking. Sometimes the chickens were treated to my leftover food, which they loved, especially lettuce. Filbert decided his favorite things were hummus and vanilla pudding. When I brought that out to the coop, everyone had to move back because they knew that was *his* treat, and he wasn't about

Filbert and Celeste

to share. He got mad if I didn't bring some type of treat out to the coop in the morning and would complain in chicken talk.

At one point, he seemed to decide he wanted to become a house rooster. If he escaped from the chicken run, he waddled as fast as he could, making his way toward the house and I had to run after to catch him and return him to the coop. Whenever he found something interesting or tasty, he would make a long, drawn-out noise, kind of like, *Aaarruurrruuuurrrrrrr*. It sounded similar to a pirate on the *Jolly Roger*, without the "Ahoy, matey" part. I mimicked him and said it right back to him because it made me laugh. Then one day at work when I noticed something interesting, I heard myself making that noise. Out loud. Everyone looked at me to see if I was okay, or if they needed to call the paramedics, because it wasn't the kind of noise someone normally would make. Embarrassed, I told them, "Oh, oops. I was making the same noise my rooster makes." They realized then that I truly was *not* okay. But they already knew that.

Filbert was now nine years old and could no longer see well. His crossed beak interfered with his being able to eat, so I used to bring him to the vet periodically to get it trimmed. They loved seeing him. It was kind of embarrassing when he let out a full-throated crow from his little kennel in the lobby. People jumped. Dogs lurched forward on their leashes to sniff at the kennel. Little kids laughed with glee.

Other roosters in the coop bullied him. He held his own for years, but now in his twilight years, the pecking order was constantly rearranged. At one time, nine roosters and many more hens coexisted in the coop, and for the most part they got along. Some scuffles, but no blood drawn, and no serious injuries. I made sure they had places to hide in case another rooster wouldn't quit. One day in the run, Spunky went for Filbert and I watched as Filbert executed a classic Teenage Mutant Ninja Turtles move to defend himself. He twirled around and flipped straight upward, legs extended and trying to nail Spunky, but he somehow leaped so high he got stuck in the bird netting above, and he was hanging upside down by his feet. I rushed to rescue him. Whenever the chickens were in their run, I make certain to never be far away because of all the predators, so I was able to disentangle him right away. He did look funny, though I decided not to laugh at him since he was so scared.

I could tell Filbert was slowing down and becoming progressively weaker, his crowing now a feeble thing. I worried he was soon to join Phoebe and the other chickens in the great chicken coop in the sky. He'd had various best friends over the years, chiefly Blanche, the Golden Polish hen, and Ginger, a small Japanese Bantam hen. One day I noticed him stumbling when he tried to walk to the food dish. He lay down and rested and I decided to drive to town to see if I could buy him some type of treat to help him feel better. I had no idea he was in such rough shape; chickens, like all birds, try to hide how sick they are. It's a prey animal thing.

When I arrived home, I immediately went to check on Filbert only to find him lying on his side. He was already gone. I set down the treats I'd purchased him and knelt next to him to brush my fingers over his feathers and cry a few tears. I don't like to say this, but the more often you see death, the less deeply affected you are. I never thought that would be the case for me, although I wager that others who have been through a lot might agree. I stood up and gazed down at my favorite rooster of all time and all I felt was empty inside. Too many deaths, too much tragedy—it tends to numb a person.

Ginger wandered over to Filbert and I watched as she nudged him repeatedly. She clucked a few times, and pulled at his feathers, trying to get him to wake up. She didn't know he was dead. She thought he was only sleeping and he'd soon be up and about to join her over at the food dish. Becoming more frantic by the second, she yanked at his feathers with her beak, pushed at his body, and tried desperately to wake up her friend. It was heartbreaking to witness. I finally had to tell her, "Ginger, he's not waking up. He's not here anymore. That's just his body. He's gone. I'm sorry." She pulled at him a few more times, and pecked at him in her frustration, then went a few feet away to sit morosely and stare disconsolately at her dead friend. People aren't the only ones who grieve. Animals, including chickens, also grieve for their lost loved ones. Perhaps in a different way, but anyone who spends enough time around animals comes to see how similar humans and animals truly are in the ways that most count. Filbert's death and Ginger's grief that day showed me this was true.

24

Flown the Coop

Over the years here, one animal after another has eventually given up the ghost. Dogs, cats, chickens, alpacas: it felt sometimes like a never-ending revolving door of expiring animals. The dogs and cats died of old age, the alpacas of injuries or illness, and the chickens? Who knows. The research I've done on chicken maladies makes clear that they are prone to all manner of unfortunate demises.

Bette was the first chicken casualty, succumbing to some type of stomach cancer. Although she couldn't stand me, she deserved to be given a decent sendoff. The day she passed, I found her on her side curled into a corner of the coop, stone-cold, and dead as a doornail. I kneeled down next to her and petted her feathers, and told her how sorry I was that she had died. Now it was on to figuring out where to bury her. Venturing into the nearby woods with a shovel, I found a likely spot for her final resting spot. Luckily the ground was soft, and I was able to dig a deep hole to foil any digging predators. I wrapped her in a funeral shroud (an old pillowcase) and gently placed her in the newly dug grave. Shedding a tear or two, I said a few words to send her on her way to the great beyond, then covered her up with dirt. Next I searched around and found several heavy rocks and large branches to place atop the grave so coyotes and raccoons didn't immediately dig her up out of the ground.

When Ursula, one of my favorite chickens, died I grieved, with many tears, much wailing, lamentations, and gnashing of teeth, because I *really* loved her. She was a tiny little black frizzle hen. Her feathers weren't like other chickens; they curled up in a haphazard fashion, thus the name "frizzle"—kind of like a chicken with a perm. She could have been considered the runt of the litter since she was half the size of the other bantam chickens in the coop, and, for whatever reason, the other chickens made her life miserable. Eventually she became ill, and I brought her into the house to hopefully help her to recover. She was the sweetest little thing, and took to sleeping in the small cat bed on the floor in the dining room. She spent her time there, and didn't normally venture anywhere else, which helped with cleaning. A bottle of hydrogen peroxide and a roll of paper towels will take care of *anything*.

One night I was sitting on the living room floor watching *Shrek* on TV. Ursula toddled out of the dining room over to me, climbed up, snuggled into my lap, and we watched the movie together. I think she enjoyed the movie; she was mesmerized. I certainly did. Once *Shrek* was over, she returned to her little bed and went to sleep.

Her illness worsened, and I didn't know how to help her other than moistening her chicken crumbles with water to make a thick "oatmeal" to keep her hydrated, and adding various herbs to treat any infection. This was far past those halcyon days of being able to afford to bring my chickens to the veterinarian at the drop of a hat. Those days were long over.

Late one afternoon I came home after being gone all day only to find her on a throw rug, dead. It was awful. I cried and cried because I loved that little chicken. Eventually I dried my tears, blew my nose numerous times, and went to find something suitable to bury her in. She was so tiny it turned out she would fit into a gallon ice cream bucket. I covered her with an old towel, placed her inside the bucket, and put on the cover, which I sealed all around with duct tape for

Ursula snuggled on her cat bed

good measure. Wanting to find a suitable resting spot for her, I walked around the yard, holding the bucket with Ursula inside in one hand and a shovel in the other. I settled on digging her grave in front of a beautiful 100-year-old oak tree. To protect her from predation after being buried, I lugged a number of landscape blocks up there and arrayed them atop her dirt-filled resting spot, making a quasi gravestone. Crying more, I told her how much I would miss her, and how I wish I could have somehow saved her.

Future chicken deaths were dealt with in a slowly devolving fashion, particularly in winter when it was impossible to dig through the snow and frozen ground. As much as I resisted it, I realized I had no choice: the dead chickens had to go out in the garbage. I felt horrible about doing it, but then I figured, *Hey, they were dead, they didn't care*. As the next chickens expired, depending on which day it was, I might have to search out which neighborhood was having garbage day because I couldn't wait a week for my own garbage day. I had nowhere else to put the corpse. First thing in the morning I would pack up the newly dead chicken in a plastic bag of some type, tie it shut, put that inside a paper grocery bag, and take off in the car with the dogs riding shotgun to find a likely garbage can to do my dirty deed. The best were in the more wooded areas a few miles from my house, with long driveways and Mc-Mansions tucked far back and not visible from the road. I'd pull up next to the garbage receptacle, look both ways, open it quickly, and pop the bag inside. I snickered a little the day Phoebe the chicken went to her final rest in a plastic BMW bag from my car dealership job at the time. I pictured someone opening the garbage can to do some dumpster diving, seeing the BMW bag, and thinking something exciting might be inside. There certainly was. A dead chicken.

One expired chicken went to its final resting place at the feed store, where the owner graciously allowed me to use their dumpster. My old boss' garbage day took care of Henri, a young rooster who died unexpectedly. I barely had him situated inside the can before the garbage truck screeched to a halt in front of me. I hoped the driver didn't take too close a look as I darted into her house, because Henri hadn't completely fit inside the plastic bag, and his long tail feathers were sticking out beyond the edge of the garbage can's cover.

Another day, another chicken death. This time it was Pebbles, a gorgeous Silver Polish. This type of chicken has feathers on their head that poof out all over. Her death was a hard one for me, too—she was really sweet. At the time of her unexpected demise, I was cat-sitting for my friend Bridget, who was out of town. It was the weekend, so no garbage days were to be found anywhere for a few days, and I certainly wasn't going to pop Pebbles into the freezer to wait for Monday, which was my garbage day.

I remembered Bridget's condo building had a community trash chute in a small room off of the second floor lobby. I tried to dissuade myself from what I was contemplating. *What would Bridget say if she knew?* I wondered. When I thought about having a dead chicken sitting out for a couple more days, my decision was made. I bundled Pebbles up in an old towel, placed her in a plastic bag and tied it securely shut, and then put that into a paper grocery bag. I pulled up to the condo and sat in my car, Pebbles in the backseat, wondering if I really was going to do it. Yes, I was. I nonchalantly walked in to the building with my bag, pretending to be delivering a bag of groceries to Granny. Pebbles was soon popped in the chute, plummeted down three stories to the dumpster, and I was down the stairs and out of the building in no time flat. I felt rather guilty about that one, and I still don't like tossing chickens out with the trash; it seems disrespectful to the dead. Poor Bridget was none the wiser…at least until she reads about it here.

I heard weird noises from somewhere when I went to feed the chickens one morning. Looking around for the source, I finally saw Ginger in her nest box, struggling, feet kicking and hitting the sides of the box, ending with her legs sticking straight up. No more movement, and I feared the worst. Rushing over to her, I exclaimed, "Oh no, Ginger! Are you dead?" Like she would answer me if she really *was* dead. Sometimes I surprise myself with the things that come out of my mouth.

I saw a slight movement. I picked her up from the nest box and placed her on the floor. Her head and neck were twisted almost upside down under her contorted body. At first I thought she had been poisoned by something she ate. I straightened out her head as best I could and noticed her eyes tracking wildly back and forth. She flopped around, struggling to get onto her feet and remain upright.

Watching her, it reminded me of the times I have experienced severe vertigo, along with my eyes darting around by themselves—something known as nystagmus. The first time it happened to me about fifteen years ago, I experienced the same thing Ginger had been doing in the nest box. I had barely awakened and was still in bed. When I moved to get up, it felt like the worst drunken bender you could ever imagine. If you've ever made the mistake of drinking too much, you might know the feeling of

Ginger

waking up in the middle of the night feeling like the room is spinning. For me that day, it was more like it was *me* spinning instead of the room, and every time I tried to sit up, I immediately ended up face down into the mattress.

This lasted for days, until I was eventually able to stumble to my car and drive to the Emergency Room. I told them I thought I must have a brain tumor. No, what was really the cause was my topmost neck vertebrae had somehow been pushed out of place, and resulted in something called cervical vertigo. It must have caused my inner ear to tell my brain, *Whoa! Something's not right here!* After two whiplash car accidents along with neck surgery in my late twenties to remove a large, benign spinal tumor, my neck is pretty well messed up. If you've ever had your lower back go out, you know how excruciating that can be. Now think of having your neck go out, and how that affects everything you do, including simply turning your head. And then add on vertigo and nausea. Ugh. Not fun, believe me.

Looking at Ginger on the floor in front of me, I thought it was worth a try to see if that's what was going on with her, too. I held her in my arms and massaged her scrawny little neck. This was kind of gross, because it put me in mind of how it feels to debone a chicken carcass from the grocery store, or handle the turkey neck at Thanksgiving. Ginger hates to be touched, but knew I was trying to help, so she let me do it. I worked out the kinks in her neck and then put her back on the floor to rest, this time thankfully sitting upright. Soon she was hungry and I made "oatmeal" for her—a slurry of chicken feed crumbles and water in a small dish. For some reason the chickens love that stuff. I held the dish in front of her so she could eat. Soon she was up and about, a bit wobbly to be sure, but still among the living. Who knew that chickens can have their backs and necks go out? She must have thrown it out when she flew up to roost the night before. I wonder if anyone else has given chiropractic treatment to a chicken, or if I'm the only weirdo who would think of it?

25

THE BOBCAT RETURNS

At dusk, I let the dogs out the back door to do their final nightly business. I always go outside with them at night because of all the predators. Almost immediately, a snarling sound came from the woods. Breezy went on point. She's a smooth-coated Collie mix, so I'm not sure why she acts like a Pointer. I had a bad feeling, so I called her back. The noise came again and I realized what it was. *Holy crap, not again*, was my thought process.

"Breezy! It's the bobcat! *Get in the house*." She actually listened and came, but I had to grab Rosebud and drag her to safety. Duke, meanwhile, decided to meander deeper into the yard. Sometimes I wonder if he thinks he's still young and could take on whatever the neighborhood predators throw at him. I don't think it would go well, but he's a stubborn dog, and you can't tell him anything. He's going to do what he wants. And since he weighs in at least at one hundred pounds, I usually am inclined to let him.

Nonetheless, I went out in the yard to get him, holding a feeble flashlight that barely illuminated the edge of the surrounding woods. Three more of those unearthly sounds quickly ensued, and I knew I had to get him (and me) out of there. Seeing me coming at him and knowing his fun was soon to be cut short, Duke tried to pull a fast one and made for the front of the house. He doesn't move too fast since he has a bad back and is arthritic, but I was able to nab him before he had gone too far. "Oh no, you don't! In the house *now!*" I said as I guided him back to the door and into the house.

Once all of us were safely inside, I turned to Breezy as she lounged on the couch, "Breezy? Was that a bobcat?" She looked at me and I could swear she made a quick nod, meaning yes. The next morning, I searched the internet for bobcat vocalizations, and finally found the noise I had heard on YouTube—two videos entitled "Bobcat Barking." The first video I watched was filmed by a guy in the woods walking with his dog. When he heard the bobcat noise, I had to laugh because he sounded exactly like me—he freaked out and turned the air blue with his swearing.

No one really believed me when I told them a bobcat was lurking around on my land. No one, that is, except my friend Bridget. She'd listen to me going on and on about it, and say, "I believe you. I don't think you're nuts. A little weird…" One day she emailed me from work and told me to Google "Bobcat sighting" in our town. *Finally,* some validation. It seems my friendly bobcat has made his way into town and been spotted a number of times lounging near the waterfall feature at Bridget's condo. So I'm not hallucinating. I don't know if that's such a good thing, though. It means there truly was at least one bobcat hanging around my house.

26

Feathers Flew

Nigel and Alfred the roosters were tight with Bianca and Lola, the cute little hens. No surprise there, since they had been hatched at the same time and grew up together. Poor Reginald and Aldrich were the odd men out and were at definite loose ends. They were too small to conquer the big girls and get some lovin', although Reggie did give it a try, only to be summarily beat up by one of those overgrown bullies, probably The Enforcer. They also didn't have any luck with the small hens, Lola and Bianca, because Nigel and Alfred chased them off if they so much as looked at their girlfriends.

One afternoon while the chickens were still living with the minis, I walked into their garage and saw Nigel pacing anxiously back and forth. Alfred and Lola were happily hanging out, but where was Bianca, the tiny white Japanese bantam hen, and Nigel's main squeeze? I'll tell you where she was—having a rendezvous with Reginald, both of them snuggled together in the straw in a corner. Nigel looked shell-shocked and didn't know what to do. He was a very handsome rooster; all creamy white, with gorgeous long, curving black tail feathers that shone iridescent purple and green in the sun. But Reggie was a hottie, too, with coppery red feathers around his head and shoulders, and the same type of iridescent feathers on the rest of his body. Plus he was an older, more experienced guy, while Nigel was a punk teenage rooster. I could see why Bianca made her move.

This was too good for me to pass up. I had to see what happened, and I waited near the door. It didn't take long, although it didn't help that I egged it on. I looked at Nigel, who was glaring over towards the two canoodling in the corner. "Nigel! Why is your girlfriend over there with Reggie? What are you going to do about it, Nigel? Your girlfriend is two-timing you. You'd better go get her."

Perhaps I should have kept my mouth shut, but it was far too tempting, and I didn't really like Nigel that much, so it was fun to needle him. He marched with a determined look over to Reggie, who was twice his size. For some reason, at that moment Nigel reminded me of Popeye right after he opened the can and ate the spinach. He launched himself at Reggie, who jumped up and ran toward Misty, who tried to bite off his head as he ran under her front legs. I guess she was on Team Nigel. Veering away from her gnashing teeth, he darted off in another direction and Nigel went for him again. Reggie managed to find a place to hide and cowered there.

Stalking over to Bianca, Nigel let her have it, chastising her in no uncertain terms. He really told her off. He strutted away, tail feathers waving, back to Alfred and Lola who were observing at a safe distance. Bianca didn't look too sorry about her dalliance. She dusted off her feathers and nonchalantly sashayed back to her friends, who all turned their backs on her. I laughed out loud. It was so much like junior high school. They all shunned poor Bianca for the next day-and-a-half. She was chickie-non-grata. She spent the time alone and forlorn. Reginald wouldn't look in her direction, worried he'd be beaten up again by Nigel. Misty and Sunny even turned on her. I had no idea chickens were so much like people.

A week after the big girls and Reggie and Aldrich moved to the outside coop, I also moved the four little ones from the minis' garage and out to the Hillbilly Hotel to live with the other chickens. I could tell Misty couldn't take living with them anymore; she was snapping at them and trying to kick them continuously. Once all the chickens were out in the Hotel, I soon noticed a red-tailed hawk perched every morning in the huge, old oak tree overlooking the small coop before the chickens come out to play, on the lookout for a nice breakfast of tasty, fresh chicken.

It was hell trying to get the four littlest chickens—Nigel, Alfred, Lola, and Bianca—to go to bed at night. They were impossible to catch in the small area of their coop and run. The little bastards were fast. I was still dealing with my sprained ankle. I no longer had the plastic cast on but trying to catch them, while not putting much weight on my injured ankle, was an ordeal. Finally I grabbed most of them, popped them in the coop, and slammed the small door shut after each one. Otherwise they would immediately jump out and the fun would start all over again. Nigel was the last holdout to be caught and he wasn't cooperating at all. He flew straight up and somehow managed to get out between the bird netting and chicken wire. I have no idea how he did that. He turned tail and ran for the woods. I yelled "You are an *idiot*! You'll be dead by morning!" Done in by chasing chickens, I went in the house to sit in front of a fan and dry the mass quantities of sweat pouring from my body. Almost recovered half an hour later, I looked outside to see him near the coop, crowing for his buddy Alfred.

It was now raining. I stalked down there and caught him somehow, bobbing and weaving on my sprained ankle. At first I chased him with a butterfly net. It didn't go well. He made tracks for the minis' garage and let me tell you, that sucker ran like the wind on his tiny legs. I chased after him, limping the whole way, as he entered their corral area. Trying to nab him, I accidentally left one of the corral panels unlatched when

I went in after him. Soon enough, I turned to see Misty cantering off to the pasture. She had seen me unlatch it and immediately went to test it by leaning her substantial weight against it. She easily pushed it open and made her escape. I quit chasing the chicken and turned to chasing a mini horse.

Swearing loudly and repeatedly, I gathered up my mini horse capture supplies: halter, lead rope, and a bucket of crack. I hobbled up to the pasture to find her. She was wandering around in the small fenced-in area, looking for the big boys, who were nowhere in sight. She didn't yet know about the new gate and expanded pasture that went all the way up the back hill to the neighboring McMansion, and I sure as hell wasn't going to tell her. The less she knew, the better. No way could I catch her if she high-tailed it for the back forty. She was wondering where her boyfriends were. I lured her by shaking the ice cream bucket of crack—it makes such an enticing sound. It worked like a charm once again, and I put on her halter and led her back to her garage.

The damn chicken was still outside, and it would soon be dark. I had to leave to be somewhere, so I hopped in my car, and as I peeled out up the driveway, I shouted, "You'll be dead before I get home, you dumb rooster!" I had left the bottom of the big garage door propped open about eight inches so he could get inside. That is, if he was smart enough. Arriving back home well after dark, I went inside the garage and turned the light on to see him asleep, perched alone up on a shelf. All was well. I glared at him before I snatched him up and stalked off to the coop to put him inside with his buddies.

The next day was unutterably hot and humid, and I knew the small coop would serve as a roasting pan if the chickens were to spend the night there.

I decided to put the three big girls and the small chickens into the much cooler tuck-under garage for the night because of the extreme heat outside. Had they been put to bed in the Hillbilly Hotel, by morning they would have been well-done. Nigel again refused to be caught, and we repeated the same dance as the previous night. He flew out between the netting and chicken wire and tore across the driveway to the minis' garage. This time he stood on top of the manure pile. I wasn't about to open the corral panel again to get at him, having learned my lesson the night before with Misty. I went to the service door and, once inside the garage, I propped up the big garage door about six inches, thinking he'd be smart enough to find his way inside again. Completely sick of dealing with him, I went in the house and told him to figure it out, I was done trying to help him.

An hour later, it was pitch black outside. I let the dogs out before I went to bed. Scared of the dark as usual, I nonetheless decided to take pity on the missing Nigel. I checked inside the garage, but he wasn't perched on a shelf, and I walked down to the small coop with a flashlight. The Hotel has two front doors (I use the term "door" loosely—how something that slapped together can be considered a door, I don't know) which swing open, along with a small flip-up door, inset on the right side door, that can be propped open. Rather than having the big doors open, the chickens were able to hop up and into the coop through the small door. I squatted down to shine the flashlight up through the small door and up into the coop. There he was. Nigel was hunched up tight in the topmost and farthest corner, scared to death since he was all alone. He must have gone in search of the other chickens, not knowing they weren't there. I swung open the big door and grabbed him. It's much easier to catch a chicken in the dark. He fought and squawked and did his best to fly away, but I had him tight to my chest. Off to the minis' garage we went, and I deposited him on the shelf where he used to sleep with his friends. "You're lucky you're alive, buddy." Owls, coyotes, raccoons—he would make a tasty treat for any of them.

The next night was cooler, and the chickens were all back in the

Nigel the rooster

Hotel. At bedtime, Nigel refused to cooperate again, and, of course, it had to be raining once again. I had securely tied the netting to the chicken wire all around their area, but that little sucker launched himself up and out of the only part I hadn't secured. He ran towards the safety of the minis' garage. I had already put the horses to bed, so the big garage door was closed, and Nigel couldn't get in. He stood on top of the manure pile frantically muttering, probably something like, *Open, sesame!* I'm not sure why I took pity on him. I really wanted to leave him out there to deal with whatever predator decided they were hungry for a chicken dinner. I'm not like that at all, but he had truly pissed me off.

I went into the minis' garage and opened the big door about six inches, again propping it up on the bottom. Then I went back out to the manure pile to talk some sense into him, telling him to go ahead and go in the garage. He actually did. I quickly climbed up and over the corral panel with my sprained ankle—so much fun!—since it was the quickest way to get the big door shut and trap him inside. Then I had to clamber back over. I limped back to open the service door to peek in at him. Misty glared at me, most likely saying, *The damn chicken is back!* Now perched up on the shelf he and his buddies had always slept on, Nigel gave me a dirty look too, as if to say, *You tricked me!* Too bad. He's lucky I didn't wring his scrawny little neck.

Having come to the long overdue conclusion there were too many chickens for my sanity, not to mention theirs, I resolved to find homes for several of them. The three big hens were first to go, and found a new life on someone's farm. I wasn't sad to see them go. I never wanted them in the first place.

Nigel and Alfred traveled up north to my niece's house to bunk with her chickens. Nigel soon left the land of the living, a victim of their hunting dog, Gunner, who had never bothered their other chickens, so I guess he didn't like Nigel either. They decided to send Alfred back to me, and he arrived a week or so later in a kennel, pissed as hell.

I tried to re-acclimate him into the flock with his old girlfriends, Bianca and Lola, and Reginald and Aldrich, the roosters. Alfred was by far the smallest of any of them, hens included, but he was always an angry little guy. His demeanor was worse after Nigel's demise. He regularly beat up the other two roosters, who took to cowering together in the corner of the run. All of us had had enough of his rage, and I put him back in with the minis in the garage to cool off one night.

The next day, I set up a separate section of the run next to the other chickens, and covered the top so he would be safe. I needed to leave around 4:30PM, and when I came home at 6:30PM, I found him dead in the yard near the small coop, feathers scattered everywhere. One of the horse boarders had shown up with her dog and was up at the pole barn with her horse. The dog trotted down to say hi to me and ambled over to sniff at Alfred's dead corpse with her head held high, totally proud of herself, with a big shit-eating grin. I knew at that moment who had offed Alfred.

The other chickens had witnessed the entire grisly murder and, traumatized by the violence, were now hiding under the coop. Right about then, the horse boarder walked back down the hill towards her truck. I pointed to the dead rooster, and shot a meaningful glance towards her dog. She said, "My dog would *never* do that!"

Right. Look at how your dog is acting, I thought. *Guilty as charged.* She was going to hop in her truck and drive off with her killer dog, leaving me to take care of disposing of the corpse, but I made her deal with the aftermath of the heinous murder, telling her, "Your dog did it, you get rid of it." I picked up poor, little, angry-no-more Alfred and handed him over to her. She began walking across the yard on her way to toss him into the woods. Not the best idea, because my dogs would drag him out and dine on him in no time, and also it was seriously disrespectful of the dead.

"Umm...no. That's not gonna work. You need to take him somewhere else." I made her put the little rooster body in her truck and drive down the road somewhere to dispose of it. I have no idea where she did the dastardly deed, and I don't want to know. She vowed she wouldn't ever bring her dog back, now apologizing to me profusely. The next day, the dog was back, trotting loose all over my yard. Sigh.

A few months later I went to feed the remaining chickens early in the morning in the Hillbilly Hotel. They were already out and about, pecking in the dirt, but I hadn't been out there yet to open the coop. I stopped in my tracks and wondered if they had somehow materialized out of the ether or something, like in the transporter on *Star Trek*. They should still have been locked securely inside the coop, waiting for me to let them out. A rooster looked up at me and gave me a dirty look, and that's when I realized: I had left the small door open all night long, for the first time ever. They could have easily been a late-night snack for a mink, a raccoon, a pack of coyotes, or whatever flavor of predator was skulking about in the small hours of the night. One of the hens looked at me reproachfully as if to say, *How could you?! We could have been killed!* I'm not sure how I forgot, as I go through the same motions every evening—round up the chickens and lock them inside their coop, and then do the same with the mini horses. Lucky for those chickens the nightly all-you-can-eat predator buffet was being held elsewhere.

It was the coldest day yet in December. In the Hillbilly Hotel, Reginald and Aldrich were now the only roosters, along with the hens, Bianca and Lola. Even though they had previously been friends, Reggie now ruled the roost and refused to let Aldrich have any quality time with the hens. Aldrich eventually had enough of it—being bullied, henpecked, rooster-pecked, what have you—it was too much for his tender soul. I went to feed them and fill their water dish. Aldrich darted over and deliberately stood under the stream of water as it poured from the bucket. He was soaked and his feathers took on a sheen of ice nearly immediately. He stood there, bedraggled, depressed, and quickly turning into a rooster-sicle. I took pity on him, scooped him up, brought him into the house to defrost, and his mood lightened considerably. I'm sure he was angling to become a house rooster, but I told him that wasn't going to happen.

All of the chickens in the Hotel soon had to move back to the much larger Coop de Ville and reacquaint themselves with the rest of the flock, because winter was finally really getting going, and they would freeze in the small coop. Once back in the big coop with the other roosters and hens, Reginald—previously the despot of the Hillbilly Hotel once Nigel and Alfred were out of his way—dropped precipitously in the pecking order because another rooster, Spunky, wasn't about to give up his reign as top rooster. Aldrich wisely stayed out of the fracas, and probably cheered on Spunky. *Karma's a bitch*, I imagined him clucking to Reggie. After a few minor dustups, peace once again reigned—if only for a short time—in the Coop de Ville.

Baby was one of the roosters out in the Coop de Ville, and Opal was his girlfriend. Only four roosters—Reginald, Aldrich, Spunky, and Baby—remained in the big coop, down from a lifetime high of nine, yes, count 'em, *nine* roosters—and Baby was *so* not getting along with any of the other three once he reached his teenage years. He beat the living crap out of Aldrich a couple of times, so it was time to find a new home for Baby. He was a sweet little rooster—thus the so-not-masculine name—as long as you weren't another rooster.

Hatched in the Coop de Ville a few years ago in the depths of winter, when he was a day old I brought him into the house and made a home for him in the bottom half of a plastic dog kennel with a chicken brooder heat lamp above to keep him warm. He would never have lived had I left him out in the coop. Hand-raised chicks for the most part grow up to be friendly and easily-handled as adults, and Baby was no exception. Before he feathered out enough out to stay warm out in the cold coop, I would sit on the floor with him in the house and he'd perch on my legs. When I sat at the dining room table, he'd hop up onto my foot, and then make his way up, hopping and flapping his wings, until he ended up in my lap, where he would take a well-deserved nap. I named him Baby because at first I thought he was a hen. He soon proved me wrong, but since he already knew his name and came to it

Nutter soaking up the rays from the heatlamp with Baby (bottom front left)

when called, I didn't rename him. I can't tell you the number of times I walked by Baby's kennel only to see my cat, Nutter, curled up next to the chick, soaking up the rays together from the infrared heat lamp. The cat didn't seem to mind when Baby pecked at him.

Not wanting the adult Baby to be lonely when he moved to his new home, I decided to also give the boot to Lola and Bianca, the tiny Japanese bantams who had lost their boyfriends, Alfred and Nigel, to separate dog attacks. Plus they didn't really get along with the other hens in the coop. While picking up supplies one day at the feed store, I asked one of the employees, Annie, if she knew of anyone who might take a rooster and a couple of hens. She said she would be interested, and a few days later I brought them to the feed store in a kennel.

The day before the big move, I sat on the ground in the chicken run with all the chickens and gently informed Baby that he would be moving to a new house. He hopped up into my lap as I sat on the ground and talked chicken talk to me. Then he flew up to perch on my left shoulder and snuggled against my head and chattered in an anxious tone some more. He was scared to go to a new place, but Lola and Bianca didn't care. Nothing bothered them.

I checked in with Annie a few days later to see how the move had gone. Turns out she also had big hens, similar to the three big hens I had recently sent to a new home. They bullied Baby unmercifully, but seemed to leave Lola and Bianca alone. Her neighbor, who owned Silkies, a fuzzy bantam breed of chicken with feathers on their heads resembling a big cottonball, took in Baby and the two hens. Her kids loved Baby since he was such a little snuggle-bunny, plus the Silkies were fine with the new additions to their flock. I miss Baby, especially because, personality-wise, he was the most like Filbert, but I have to say the Coop de Ville is much calmer without his added testosterone.

27

GOING BATTY

I opened the front door on a bright, sunny afternoon ready to step outside, and that's when the bat sitting in the raised brick flowerbed next to the door hissed at me, sharp teeth bared as it reared back, ready to launch itself at me. I hastily reconsidered, shut the glass storm door, and watched it watch me. Rosie and Breezy were hanging out on the steps near it. The minis were in their corral in the front yard, doing their civic duty and mowing my front lawn down to microscopic lengths. The bat took flight, did a couple of circles and landed back amongst the flowers.

Worrying about the dogs possibly being bitten by the bat, even though their rabies shots were current, I dashed to the back porch door and called for them to come into the house. Once they were safe, I realized the minis were still outside, forty feet from the rabid flying rodent, and their rabies shots were *not* current.

I don't know if many horses are vaccinated against rabies, but when my minis were still loose in the big pasture, I made sure they had their rabies shots. I've seen too many rabid creatures in my years here. Once the minis had moved into the safety of the detached two-car garage, I let their vaccinations slide. Now they were once again in the crosshairs, munching away without a clue to the danger they were in. I'm not sure what a rabid mini horse might be like—probably better behaved than usual—but I didn't want to find out.

The sun was beating down on that hot summer day. I peeked out the front storm door, but the bat was nowhere in sight. I wasn't about to go out there defenseless, and I suited up in my armor to rescue the maidens in distress—Misty and Sunny. Two pairs of jeans. Heavy boots. Winter parka with hood tightened securely so only the top part of my face was exposed. Safety glasses for protection in case the vile creature went for my eyes. Thick mittens. A broom substituted for my trusty baseball bat as I figured it would be easier to knock a winged predator out of the sky with a broom.

Now fully impervious to airborne assault, I returned to the door and eyeballed the surrounding area…still no bat. Once outside, I dashed down to the garage to grab the minis' halters and lead ropes, then ran over to their mobile corral, opened it, and went in, sweating buckets in my getup. The minis didn't want to be caught, as more grass remained

The minis mowing the lawn in the portable corral—
their garage is on the top right side

to gobble. Their corral was ten feet by ten feet square, and I chased them around for the longest time until I finally cornered one, got the halter on her and tied her up to the metal corral. Then it was on to the next pursuit, sweat nearly blinding me. Eventually I caught the other one, all the while scanning the sky for incoming. Opening the corral, I untied the first mini and dragged both of them to the garage, telling them to hurry up or we'd all get rabies and die a horrible, painful death. Needless to say, I never saw the bat again. Yay. Let's hope I never see another one.

A few days later I noticed two puncture marks inside my left arm near the wrist. They looked fresh, and barely scabbed over. Did the bat somehow get me? Or had I clumsily run into something, say, two equidistantly spaced sharp nails, and not remembered it? This type of thing happens more often than I care to admit—the not remembering, not the sharp nails. Although I do tend to step on them every so often. Good thing my tetanus shots are current.

I have no idea how I got them, or where those wounds came from, but thankfully I never developed rabies, and never started foaming at the mouth—other than when I'm yelling at one animal or another, of course, which is par for the course—and I'm still alive and kicking. I bet the damn bat isn't, so that's good.

28

Nine Lives

The cats nearly never are allowed outside because of all the critters that would delight in making short work of them. One day I took pity and let one of the cats, Luna, run free with the dogs, who were sprawled on the front steps. She had been mewling piteously in the foyer, gazing longingly out the glass storm door to the unattainable wonders of the front yard. I let her out and kept watch, sitting in the living room chair nearest the window, holding a nice hot mug of coffee, with Nutter on my lap. Before long, through the picture window, I noticed a bald eagle, incoming from the north, flying low. I slammed the mug down on the end table, sloshing coffee all over the place, including on Nutter and me. Unceremoniously tossing Nutter off my lap as he protested loudly, I then skidded at full speed across the wood floor with hands outstretched until I hit the wall. I tore down the steps to the front door and fumbled with the deadbolt. Finally getting the damn door open, I frantically looked for Luna. She was right there, on the sidewalk. She was also in full view of any flying predators, namely the eagle. Practically levitating down the front steps, I ran to snatch her up from certain death. Luna now safely in my arms,

I looked up to see the eagle forty feet above us, glancing down at the snack he had hoped to swoop down on. Whew! We dodged a bullet that time.

Not learning a thing from this and, to tell the truth, completely unaware of how closely she had cheated death, a few days later Luna was again scratching at the door to go out. This time it was the back door. It was a semi-nice late fall day and I let her outside then followed to keep an eye on her. The three dogs, Breezy, Rosie, and Duke hung out with us. Rambo, the guy I let hunt on my land, showed up for a spot of deer hunting and he walked past on his way to his deer stand in the woods, way out in the back forty. He stopped to chat, and was surprised to see a cat on the loose, as he knows all too well from all the photos on his trail camera how many predators call my property home. Jokingly, I pointed at Luna and said, "Eagle bait." Not two seconds later, an eerie bird noise came from the woods edging the backyard. "What was *that?*" I said to Rambo. We both scanned the higher branches of the trees and saw a huge hawk scoping out Luna as she scampered blissfully unaware in the backyard. Rambo looked at me, then threw a meaningful glance at Luna, and I ran to scoop her up to live another day. Once again, Luna had no clue whatsoever. It must be nice to be blissfully unaware of all the dangers. I wish I could be like that.

One day Rambo was out in the woods, in his happy place, hunting. His truck was parked off the driveway in my front yard. I saw Breezy jumping up onto the back bumper, trying valiantly to get into the truck bed, although it was far too high for her to manage. I walked down there and looked into the bed of the truck and saw what I thought was a toy. Not sure why someone as serious a hunter as Rambo might be packing *a toy* in his truck, I was curious enough to pick it up, only to realize I was holding the severed head of a mallard duck. I gingerly set it back down without screaming or puking and said to no one in particular, "That is *really* gross" as I wiped my hands on my jeans. I thought of

Rambo, driving all over creation with a decapitated duck head in his truck bed. I never asked him about it. I decided I didn't really want to know.

Kerwin, another of my cats, has an odd sense of humor. He's a practical joker. I have no idea how old he is, as he was a rescue cat. One day several years ago, I walked into the feed store to buy hay for the minis, and walked out with a cat, similar to what happened when I got Breezy. I certainly didn't *want* another cat. I certainly didn't *need* another cat. Yet somehow this cat managed to finagle me into adopting him. Sitting near the door at the feed store was a Seal Point Siamese, with the most beautiful ice blue eyes, looking at me. I walked away and went up to the counter to pay for whatever else I was buying that day. The girl working there saw the cat staring at me and said, "Oh, you should adopt him." She went over, picked him up, and brought him to me. He snuggled in my arms like he belonged there and wouldn't leave me. So of course he went home with me. After his arrival here, he fit right in with the rest of the furry mafia, with no major dust-ups to speak of with the other cats, and all was well.

His weird sense of humor didn't take long to emerge. Like many other cats, he delighted in clambering into every paper bag he could find. He's not a small cat, but he had no problem crawling into grocery bags and hiding out, only his eyes visible. The weird part was when he crawled into any other size of paper bag, including those far too small for his bulk. I'm talking the size of the paper bags the liquor store uses for wine bottles, or the ones you'd use to pack your kid's lunch. No matter the size, Kerwin did his best to crawl into it. More times than not, I'd hear a ripping sound as the sides of the bag gave way to his tunneling. He would then lay in the middle of the destruction and purr.

Paper bags were one thing, but give him the plastic bag a six-pack of paper towels comes in? Heaven, sheer heaven. Whenever I have a new package of paper towels, I tear the plastic only enough to remove one roll at a time and then set the rest on the floor next to the fridge. Once several rolls have been removed, Kerwin burrows inside and gazes out at the world through crinkled plastic. I was worried he might suffocate, but he hasn't, and he can back out whenever he wants to. He never wants to…it's *much* too fun.

When an unsuspecting dog wanders past, he lunges forward, encased in the plastic, and attacks with outstretched paws. Breezy jumped straight into the air the first time Kerwin punked her, and it made me laugh out loud. Breezy deserved it—she's the ultimate practical joker. Another time, Nutter walked by and noticed Kerwin peering out from inside the plastic. He came to a dead stop and glared daggers at Kerwin, probably telling him in cat language, *Don't you even think of it!* Kerwin couldn't take the suspense and leaped forward in attack. A huge tussle broke out, and they rolled around on the floor, Kerwin still in the plastic. I had to break them up and toss out the plastic, since it was in shreds.

I somehow ended up the owner of a pink pencil eraser in the shape of a brain. Not being a pencil user—in fact I hate the things with a passion due to the horrid scratching noise they make on paper—I decided to find some use for it. Kerwin was wandering around, looking for mischief to get into and I tossed the brain at him. It bounced a few times and he looked down at it and then up at me, wondering what new lunacy I was engaged in.

Snickering a bit, I said, "Oh no, you lost your brain! Where's your brain, Kerwin?"

He batted it around as I walked away to do something else. Later, while cleaning, I found it under the end table and tossed it at him. "I found your brain!" I cackled.

Clearly humoring me, after I tossed it towards him and it bounced enticingly, he played with it to make me happy. His brain soon went missing again and was out of commission for weeks. I don't know how he made do without a brain. One day I checked under the couch for something I dropped. I didn't find that, but lo and behold, I came up with Kerwin's brain. "Hey, Kerwin! I found your brain! *Thank God,* now you have a brain." He looked at me with his lip slightly curled. Perhaps he found it humorous. He has an odd sense of humor. Or else he was entirely sick of my shenanigans. I thought it was funny, but I'm easily amused.

Kerwin inspecting his newly rediscovered brain

29

It's Time to Go

Although I loved seeing the big horses out in the pasture, and walking up with my coffee in the morning to sit and hang out with them, eventually I decided that horse boarding wasn't for me. You'd think it would be simple, and no work was involved, other than opening the envelope to find the monthly boarding check. This may be true for other boarding stables, but it didn't work out that way for me, and I was aggravated with some of the things that happened. I was also contemplating selling part of my land and building a new house closer to the road, and I doubted a new owner would want to inherit horse boarders. Plus big horses really do a number on the land, their big hooves tearing everything up and trampling it flat. The herd of beef cattle we had when I was a kid wasn't even close to that destructive. I sent the boarders their thirty-day notice and informed them they needed to find a new boarding facility for their horses. I loved the horses—they were really nice horses, and I was sad to see them go.

Don't get me wrong—the boarders were good people, and helped me out a lot around here. I know I got on their nerves with some of the things I did, too. I think the biggest problem was lack of communication, on both sides, as well as differing ideas about how things should be done.

When I was growing up, this property was thirty-five acres; after my mom died, my brother and I split it down the middle, and I was left with half. As a kid, I wandered nearly daily all over the land, sitting out in the pasture to do my homework in the warm breeze, and exploring every nook and cranny of this property. My best friend when I was a child lived over on the other side of the big hill in my pasture—down in the valley behind where the McMansion now looms at the crest of the hill. She and I sat for hours on that hill, dreaming and talking. We loved to roll down the hill, lying flat on the ground, tucking our heads into our arms, then launching ourselves forward and barreling down to the bottom. We could do that all day long. It was so much fun. Even today as a middle-aged woman, I would do it again in a heartbeat. The only thing that stops me is that the people in the McMansion would surely have no choice but to send the guys in the white coats with the straightjackets to deal with that crazy neighbor. They've somehow held off from doing it during the other odd incidences involving me they've observed from their lofty perch—the restraint they've demonstrated is rather admirable, I'd say.

Now that I've been living here again as an adult, it seemed to be overkill to have this much land and no longer enjoy it. I have ventured out and explored a few times, but I have such a fear of coyotes now that it wasn't much fun to be out there while always watching my back. They might not attack me, but the coyotes around here are incredibly bold and not afraid of people at all. I've been face-to-face with enough of them now to realize they don't consider people to be a threat. Although they have eventually run off each time I've challenged them with my handy baseball bat and my cuss words, I worry that one of these times I'll meet up with the alpha coyote of the pack, and he won't back down. I've seen him a few times—he's huge. A trapper told me once that coyotes around here are mixed with timber wolves. I believe it. It looked like a wolf, and had the same intelligence in his eyes. The other coyotes all had crazy eyes. This meant the alpha coyote was not only smart like a wolf, but as cunning as a coyote: a lethal mix.

If I ever was attacked, I wouldn't dare run—it would be on me in a heartbeat because they move *fast*. I'd have to face it and fight it. It's come close to that a few times already. I seriously hope that day never comes. Talking to a hunter one day, we discussed coyotes and I told him how bold they were at my house, and how I worried that one day, I'd be forced to fight one. He said if that happens, and it comes at me, to ram my fist down its throat and hold on tight with my other hand until it suffocates. I don't know if I would ever do something like that but, knowing myself, if it came down to it, I would do whatever it took to protect myself. I've done it enough times protecting my dogs. You'll excuse me if I have a raging case of coyote PTSD, and don't feel like I'm able to enjoy my land.

The horses' moving day had arrived, and they were soon to be on their way to their new home, a farm nearby. I had visited them in the pasture many times in the days before they left, saying my goodbyes, shedding a few tears, hugging them, and kissing their noses. I'd broken the news to Sunny and Misty that their boyfriends would no longer be living here, and they wouldn't be able to look up the hill at them and flirt long distance. The minis were sad when they heard the news, because they really loved those boys. I thought the boarders would lead their horses over to let the minis say goodbye, but they walked them past without a second glance, and off they went. Misty whinnied in lament and pushed against her corral panel. Sunny ate her hay, pragmatic as always, but Misty stood forlornly watching as they went up the

Duke on the front steps

driveway and out of her life. When I went out that night before dark to put them to bed and close the big garage door, Misty was staring up at the pasture, looking for the big horses who were now gone. I felt bad for her; she was so sad. I let her know that she would still be able to see them whenever they were ridden past out on the road. The dogs also were sad, and couldn't figure out why no horses came to greet them when they ran out into the pasture to say hi to them.

A month later, the dogs and I were sitting outside in the early evening, listening to the chorus of bullfrogs in the ponds. The air was quiet and still and suddenly we heard a horse whinny several times, off in the direction of where the boys were now living. We all perked our ears and looked off to the west; we knew it was one of the boys. Suddenly, Duke lumbered to his feet and made his plodding way across the backyard. I knew why—he was on his way to look for his horse friends. He thought they were back home, since he had heard one of them whinny. Jumping up, I followed him since it was that prime coyote time of night. I was right—he was headed to the pasture. Rosie and Breezy took off in pursuit. We wandered about in the paddock while Duke sniffed and searched for his friends. I felt sorry for him and said, "They moved, Duke. They don't live here anymore. You might see them out on the road sometime."

Three times I led him out of the paddock and he turned back to search through the tall weeds, hoping to find them. Rosie had made her way close to the back woods and, through the trees, I caught a flash of brown—a coyote? No, it was a deer standing and watching us, its ears pricked up. It wasn't afraid of us as we wandered about.

Later that summer, I took Duke for a walk out on the road. In the distance, I saw two horses being ridden towards us. As they neared, Duke perked up and wagged his tail. It was two of his horse buddies, and they touched noses with him in greeting. As we continued on our walk, I knew Duke was happy about seeing his friends again.

30

Heaven Is a Hammock

The middle of November, and the weather had been gorgeous—more like mid-September, with temps in the 60s and sunny days. We hadn't even had a freeze yet, not to mention snow, which is completely out of character for the frozen tundra otherwise known as Minnesota. Not that I was complaining. The wonderful weather allowed Breezy and me to log many more days in the hammock than we normally would be allotted. The other shoe was soon to drop, though, as weather reports called for the temperature to plummet, and snow was set to arrive the next night.

Knowing our idyllic days were severely numbered, I turned to Breezy as we walked about the yard on our daily livestock feeding routine and said, "This is our last chance to hit the hammock, Breezy. We'd better take advantage of it." I had briefly flirted with the novel idea of bringing the hammock setup inside, to a spare bedroom. I could hang a spare chicken brooder light equipped with a 250-watt infrared bulb above the hammock, to double as a "sun." Nah. Too much work. And a little *too* weird, even for me.

Soon after the mini horses and chickens were happily chowing down, Breezy and I retired to the hammock. I brought along a book, of course. You can't simply lazily swing the day away when you're in a hammock. You have to do something *constructive,* like read.

The sun was now at a much lower angle in the sky than in summer, and the trees over by the pasture blocked it somewhat as it made its way to the west. The petunias near the house were still blooming, and a dragonfly darted past—unheard of for November in Minnesota.

Breezy happily ensconsed on the hammock

Things got rather chilly when the sun hid behind the gathering clouds and the wind picked up to a brisk 10–15 mph. Breezy and I didn't care, though. We were snuggled up under a nice, thick blanket. I am nothing if not prepared for these hammock ventures. Only my face was exposed, as well as my hands as I held the book above me to read. My nose was cold, but that was about it. Breezy was curled up along my side, and that part of me was toasty warm. We whiled away the afternoon hours in companionable silence, happily ensconsed in our beloved hammock until almost dusk. Things were becoming downright nippy by that point. I nudged Breezy awake, "Okay, all done with hammocking until next spring!" and I started to sit up.

Not so fast, I imagined her saying, as she practically leaped on top of me, holding me down with her front legs, her chest splayed across my upper body. I couldn't wrestle my way free—she's too heavy. Her face was right in mine and the look on her face cracked me up—*Oh no, you don't! You'll get up when I say you can.* She was determined to eke out a few more minutes of hammock time.

Then she saw a squirrel and her attention was briefly diverted. Deciding whether to chase it, she wiggled away and nearly tumbled off the edge. I saw my chance and tried to wrest myself free of her and attempted to sit up. Instantly she whirled around and pinned me back down, flat on my back. It wasn't until nearly full dark that I was able to wrestle myself away and hop off onto the ground. This time she let me, because even she was getting cold.

A few days after the miniscule snowstorm, I walked around the yard, picking up the last bits of summer to store them away in the garage until next spring. Garden ornaments, gazing balls, and planters all went to their winter resting spot. Last was the hammock frame. Breezy rounded the corner of the house as I was disassembling the last few pieces. The look of sorrow on her face was priceless.

She really *loves* her hammock.

31

The Cone of Shame

Outside once again at 7:30AM in late February, and it was barely light. Of course I was out *there* rather than in my comfy, warm bed, since I had to stand guard over Duke and Breezy as they did their business. Rosie had sadly passed away from her cancer a few weeks before, and all of us were still getting used to not having her around. I held my baseball bat and scanned the perimeter of the yard, looking for danger. Breezy trotted over to the edge of the woods near the steep hill down to one of the ponds, cocked her head, and sniffed loudly at something. She was mighty interested in whatever it was. I should have known what was coming, because that's the same place she's gone in chase of coyotes several times in the last few years.

Unfortunately, I was caffeine-deprived, as I hadn't yet made coffee, and didn't connect the dots until it was far too late. She was off like a shot over the crest of the hill and disappearing down towards the pond at full speed. I yelled for her and took off across the snow, clad once again in that poor winter shoe choice otherwise known as Crocs.

Once I made it to the driveway, if things proceeded as they had in the past, I would launch myself full tilt up the driveway and Breezy and

I would face off the big, bad coyote together. Because it *had* to be a coyote. Were this a deer running in the woods, tremendous crashing sounds would have ensued, because those suckers don't run silently. A coyote runs silently. And fast.

Skidding to a halt, I realized the driveway was glare ice and my Crocs were no match for it. I didn't feel like turning myself into a human bowling ball that early in the morning. I glanced up to the yard to be sure that Duke was safely near the house and then, hefting the bat, I yelled for Breezy to get her butt back home. I ran across the snow to see if I could make it down on to the pond itself, but a tree had fallen across the path down the hill, and I doubted I could clamber over it. Then I saw them. Two coyotes raced together across the pond, away from the direction they had been chased by Breezy. I raised my baseball bat and swore at them. I may have also invited them to come my direction so I could bash their evil little brains in, but they didn't give me the time of day. The thing about coyotes, and predators in general, is you can't turn your back to them—it shows submission, weakness, and fear. You need to establish dominance quickly and hope the damn thing won't fight back. At least that's the general idea. It's worked for me in the past, and my huge vocabulary of swear words has also served me in good stead.

The coyotes disappeared into the far woods and I turned in search of Breezy. I was beginning to be really concerned—I hadn't heard any barking or snarling or general fighting noises. It was a quiet winter morning and if there had been a knock-down, drag-out fight I should have heard *something*. Peering back up the driveway, I saw Breezy. She was limping badly and stopped every few feet to lift her right leg and lick at it. Her inside elbow was torn completely open to the muscle, and a large flap of her skin and fur were hanging below it. Thankfully there wasn't blood spurting all over the place. I helped her to the house and collected Duke and we all went inside, but not before I said, "You *never* listen. I've told how many times not to go after coyotes—did you listen? No. And now you're paying the price. And so am I, because I needed my money to pay bills, and instead I'm going to have to pay a vet to sew you up."

It was a Saturday, and I knew no veterinarians opened until 9AM and we had to wait. I tried to bandage her leg, but she was in too much pain and wouldn't let me near it. I looked at her and said, "You'll have to suffer then. You're going to need surgery on that. Thanks, Breezy. I had money and now I don't, thanks to you not listening to me." I went to the kitchen to make coffee and wished I had something stronger to pour into it. You might think I was being too hard on her—after all, she had just been hurt by coyotes—but this kind of crap has happened too many times with her, and I was fed up. How much stress can one person take? A hell of a lot, if it's me. To be honest, this level of stress is unsustainable. Either I need to change how I react to all the stuff that happens around here, or I pack it in and leave. It's gotten to that point a number of times.

She spent the entire morning at the vet's having surgery on her leg to sew everything up. They told me later the coyotes had missed her artery by less than an inch—she would have bled out had her artery

Breezy wearing the Cone of Shame, hanging out with Donald the goat

been severed. We arrived home and all the cats and Duke immediately crowded around to check out Breezy's new fashion statement—the Cone of Shame—otherwise known for some odd reason as an Elizabethan Collar. She hated that cone, but too damn bad. I hated having to pay another vet bill, so we were even.

Breezy Conehead—that's what I took to calling her. Three times that first day after she came home from the vet, when we went outside with her safe on a leash, seven deer were by the fence watching her and she couldn't go get them. *Bwahahahaha.* It's like they knew she was out of commission and couldn't chase them, and they had to rub it in. Repeatedly.

32

Revenge is Sweet

Sitting in the dining room once again at my computer, I searched online for tundra swan sounds to identify what type of large white birds had been in the flock that had flown over my house that day. Yup. I was right—they *were* tundra swans, on their spring migration to the far northern reaches of Canada and their nesting grounds. I absolutely love seeing and hearing the tundra swans fly high overhead each spring and fall on their migration.

Eventually I came across several websites with all manner of wild animal calls. Red fox "bark"—yup, I've heard that one—it sounds like a woman screaming. Not exactly fun to hear *that* when you're outside alone after dark. I didn't pay attention to what my cats and dogs were doing while I played animal sound after animal sound, not until I played the coyote howls. The cats, who had been lazing in their beds in the bay window, flattened themselves and jerked their heads around in a panic, looking for the coyote in the house. Breezy ran to the window and barked non-stop, jumping up and down, thinking the coyotes were right outside the house and she could rumble with them. I laughed out loud that she could be that easily tricked.

Next came the barred owl call. The cats nearly had a heart attack when they heard that sound right next to them. An evil laugh or two from me, and we were on to the bobcat growl and then its purr. One cat came running to see where the big kitty was. Breezy was still barking at the window, and I thought, *What the heck*, and played the wolf pack howl, thinking that would have to be scarier than the coyote yips and howls. Not even close.

I guess I'd never heard what wolves sound like before—it was a low-pitched, deep-throated ululation—spooky in the extreme. An image of me in the North Woods alone in a flimsy tent popped into my mind, a pack of hungry wolves loping in from the surrounding forest, intent on leaping upon me and tearing me limb from limb.

Glad I was sitting in the safety of my dining room and not somewhere deep in the woods at the mercy of a pack of wild, slavering animals, I looked around to see the cats wide-eyed, ears flat to their heads, and completely silent, wondering what new manner of foul beast had invaded our home. They obviously didn't much care for wolves. I suddenly realized Breezy was no longer barking. In fact, she was now completely calm and had strolled slowly and sedately over to the couch, climbed onto it, and curled up for a nap. What the heck? Coyotes send her into a frenzy but the much more cunning and intelligent wolf calms her down? That was too weird, and I played more owl sounds to get the cats going again. "Revenge is sweet," I cackled. "This is for all the times you little suckers leaped on me en masse in the middle of the night and stuck your whiskers in my face, whining for me to fill your food bowl. Take *that* you little fiends!"

33

Fun and Games

Over the years, I've taken in various animals needing a new home—probably more than I should have. I've allowed the chickens to have babies, making for far too many chickens. I let people dump their unwanted cats and dogs and even a hamster on me. I allowed the three big hens to be offloaded on me, until I eventually found them a new home. Periodically I pared down the flock and the herd. I sold the llama. The alpacas were no longer here either.

One day not long ago, I was talking to an acquaintance only to learn he had announced to someone who needed to find a home for some unwanted chickens, "Oh, Sue would be *happy* to take your chickens. No problem. You can drop them off anytime." I was rendered completely speechless that he thought it was okay to speak for me, and it wasn't until the next day that I regained my voice, telling this person, "I will *not* be an animal sanctuary any longer. No one is offloading any more animals on me. I have enough animals of my own as it is." Soon after, a neighbor called and asked if I would board his four goats for the winter, and he would be happy to pay me. Although the added income would have been helpful, I have finally come to the long and painfully overdue realization that I don't *need* any more work. I don't *need* to make someone else's life easier at my own expense. I told him no.

Several years ago, it was time once again to say goodbye to another rooster. He was a good-looking guy, but with hugely raging hormones. It's a good thing I don't have feathers or I might have been the next chick on his list. His name was Lancelot and he was incredibly handsome but, oh my, what a jerk. He treated the ladies like crap. On and off and on, he leaped atop the hens all day long, like an Energizer Bunny. Several of the hens' back feathers were worn off from all the boinking, and their skin was becoming raw. He also refused to get along with the other roosters. It was time to find him a new home. I kept working on the veterinary assistant where I had brought Filbert for his beak trimming to see if he would possibly take Lance. The vet tech loved Filbert—why wouldn't he also love one of Filbert's great-great-grandchildren? Unfortunately, the tech was far too smart for that and he never fell for my pitch.

Searching for a new home for Lancelot, I formally placed him up for adoption on the local Twin Cities Chickens Google group. Yes, there truly is such a thing, where chicken aficionados exchange advice and knowledge. As part of his listing, I asked only that whoever took him not make him into a McNugget. Those were my exact words. I never got any takers. It's difficult to find a home for a rooster. It would help if they didn't crow all the time (even in the middle of the night) and fight with the other roosters. Other than that, roosters are great.

Finally I mentioned Lancelot needing a new home on one of my innumerable trips to the feed store, and learned that one of their previous employees was willing to take him. She owned a petting zoo, with a mini horse, tons of chickens, a llama, and a huge tortoise. I bundled him up inside a small dog kennel and brought him to her house. We walked to the backyard where at least a hundred hens of all shapes, sizes, and colors were darting to and fro. Glancing down at Lancelot. I could tell he was envisioning a very busy romantic life with all of these hot new chickies. He greedily eyed the milling throngs of future conquests, probably deciding where to begin. I knew he was exactly where he needed to be.

Animals are a lot of work. The more animals you have, the more work it is. You'd think I'd have grasped that concept from the get-go, but I didn't. It took years of traumatic experiences, tons of back-breaking labor, massive amounts of stress, and scads of money down the drain before it finally got through my thick noggin. You have to wonder why I've put myself through all of it. I certainly do. Not to mention why I'm still putting myself through it.

One morning I couldn't get in the minis' garage to feed them because the doorknob on the small service door wouldn't work. It didn't even turn. Getting in through the big garage door was out, too, because I don't have a key to the outside lock—that was probably lost sometime by my dad back in the 1960s.

I went back to the house for something to help me break into the garage. First I tried to smash the flimsy wood door down with a hammer, mostly because I was so mad. It didn't work, but it made me feel better to get my aggression out. I did manage to put a hammer-sized hole right through the door, but that was no help whatsoever. Eventually I decided to try the move they use in cop movies—step back, lift up my leg, and launch a martial arts kick at the door. The door didn't budge, but my knee certainly screamed in pain.

The only other way in was the window. I've had to go in through the window in the past to get in that garage, and I knew it could be done. Grabbing a ladder from the house, I placed it under the awning window which thankfully was already propped open to the inside by a measly bungee cord attached to a nail. The window opening was about two feet tall and three feet wide—hopefully wide enough for me to crawl my sorry ass through. Gripping the outside of the window trim with one hand, I climbed the ladder, which swayed precariously in the soft dirt. I tend to fall off kitchen chairs and break my thumb—did I really think I could accomplish this new climbing task and come out unscathed? I was sure as hell going to try.

I took a deep breath and launched my body over the edge of the open window, dragging myself until the front part of my body was inside, and my hips and legs were dangling on the outside. Doing my best not to topple off the window ledge and land face first into the manure pile so thoughtfully placed by a mini horse directly under the window, I wriggled forward, scissor-kicking my legs to give myself some momentum. No way would I be able to twist around like a pretzel in the window opening so as to have my legs land first. Seriously—I'm over fifty. It's not like I'm as agile as I was years ago. I balanced there on the window, thinking about my next step. Noticing a metal cabinet to my left, I reached over and grabbed it. Its surface was below me, and I was able to inch over far enough to crawl atop it.

I looked over to see Misty and Sunny watching me, probably taking bets with each other about whether I'd land in the manure or not. I can't tell you how much entertainment I've provided for those two over the years. Far more than they've provided me, that's for sure. Once safely on top of the cabinet, I made my way carefully to the floor and walked over to the door. The knob wouldn't work from the inside either, but I found a screwdriver on a shelf and pried it into the jamb where the lock met the wood and jimmied the door open. My stunning handyman skills came to the fore, and I successfully replaced the doorknob.

It only took me an hour, too, since the stupid thing refused to cooperate and I kept dropping the screws.

Christmas Day, and you'd think there'd be a blizzard, or at least a snowstorm. No, there wasn't. Instead, we had a thunderstorm, with several inches of rain pouring down in sheets. In Minnesota? In late December? *Really?* The snow on my driveway turned to sheets of ice. In the morning I carefully ventured out, walking with baby steps, and filled a five-gallon bucket with salt and spread it on the portion of the driveway going up the hill with a steep drop off between the two ponds on each side. I have a long driveway and it's only about twelve feet wide at that part. You have to be very careful driving whenever fresh snow falls or when the delightful ice appears. Years ago my sister-in-law drove down the driveway and her car slid off the edge. Luckily she hit a small tree, which stopped her car from flipping end-over-end into the ice-covered pond. I've almost been sucked off the edge myself right there too many times to count. White-knuckle driving, every single time.

The salt was all gone and there'd barely been enough to make a dent in the ice on the driveway. In order to get more salt or sand, I'd need to drive up that driveway and make a run to town. No way in hell was I about to tackle that icy driveway the way it was. There had to be something else I could use to give traction to my car. Heaving a deep sigh, I baby-stepped my way all the way back down the driveway, went into the minis' garage, and shoveled fresh manure and straw into a plastic sled, dragged that up the driveway, and spread manure on the ice. I didn't have a choice. I needed to get out of my driveway to buy grit to lay on the rest of the driveway, which is a tenth of a mile long—a heck of a lot of ice and, while the minis might produce a lot of manure, it's not as much as I'd need. Plus I wasn't too excited about dragging horse crap up the driveway all day.

Hopping in my car, I crossed my fingers, said a little prayer, and put it in drive, creeping like a snail up the driveway. I made it to the top of the hill with only a few scary moments. Then I had to brave the end of the driveway, where it slopes down to the gravel road. It's always horrible when it's icy. My car slid out of control straight down into the middle of the road. Thankfully no other cars were passing by right then or I would have T-boned them. The gravel road itself wasn't in much better shape, although the city had laid down a smidgeon of gravel and salt down the center, but none on the sides. I kept to the middle of the road, crawling along, and finally made it to the highway, which was blissfully free of ice.

At the feed store, I bought two fifty-pound bags of grit and headed back home. More stress-inducing sliding commenced once the car was on the ice-covered gravel road. When I reached my driveway, I parked out on the road and lugged a bag of grit with me as I walked down the driveway, scattering grit on the worst parts of the ice. I walked the entire tenth-of-a-mile driveway, lugging the heavy bags and scattering the grit.

The temperature at the time was a balmy twenty degrees (above zero for once) although the 40–50 mph wind gusts cut right through the jeans I was wearing. The wind chill made it feel like thirty-below-zero. Frozen through-and-through after being out there for half-an-hour, I headed back to my car and drove down to my house. I was feeling rather crabby, to put it mildly. I don't mind winter; actually I prefer it to summer. I'm weird that way. What I *don't* like is having to deal with the stressful parts of winter: worrying about sliding off the road, or slipping on the ice and falling on my head (a thoroughly enjoyable experience I had two years ago—the sound when the back of my head hit the ice was like an overly ripe watermelon—luckily I didn't have a concussion).

Winter is the sun sparkling like millions of glittering diamonds on new fallen snow; the crisp, cold air; the beautiful silhouettes of the bare trees; the silence at night when you can actually hear the snowflakes falling and the owls calling to each other in the distance. I love winter. It's peaceful. I sometimes sit out on the front step when it's freezing cold and allow myself to be enveloped in the solitude and serenity of winter. It recharges me. Summer—that sucks me dry. I want to hibernate. If that makes me weird, so be it.

Misty, Sunny, and Donald were engaged in happily snacking on their hay on a gorgeous early September day. Meanwhile, I was raking and shoveling manure and soiled straw bedding nearby. After being at it for far too long, I took a break, leaned on my shovel and said, "It's good that I'm cleaning out your garage." Misty stopped chewing, looked up at me, and I could swear she said, *It's about time.* We looked at each other silently for a few more seconds. I went back to mucking out the stall, and she went back to munching.

One day I was at Bridget's condo, babysitting her cat Lucy while she was out of town. Lucy and I hung out together on the balcony, me reading a book and sipping an iced tea, Lucy stretched out on a chair, sunning herself. Suddenly it hit me. Something was different. I looked up, trying to figure out what. Finally I realized—it was *me.* I was relaxed. I had no responsibilities. I looked around, realizing my life could be like this all the time. No stress. No traumatic coyote incursions. No shoveling. No taking my life into my hands driving up an icy driveway. *What would it be like,* I wondered. *What would it be like to feel like this every day?*

Who knows, one of these days I just might do it—shuck the hobby farm lifestyle, and find good homes for the mini horses, the goat, and the chickens. Idly thinking about it one afternoon, I happened to look up my property online on Zillow.com. It described my house, the acreage, and had an aerial view of the house. I zoomed in on it and for some reason it didn't look right. Then I realized what was wrong—the photo was of the pasture, and the "house" was *the mini mansion*—the slapped-together, ramshackle horse shed. They must think it's superior to the shack I actually live in. I could not stop laughing. It was too damn funny.

And now, after all these years of wondering what I would do, it finally happened. Untold years of my going outside with the dogs after dark and scanning my flashlight's beam continuously along the edge of the woods, looking for the reflection of eyes. I always wondered how I would react. Now I know. A cold winter's night, and of course the dogs needed to go outside once again before bed. Putting on my parka and boots, I grabbed the flashlight and we went out to the backyard. While the dogs sniffed around close to the house in the freshly fallen snow, I did my usual routine with the flashlight. Something caught my eye, and I moved the beam of light around a little. I'd never seen anything in all these years, and I wasn't paying too much attention. Then I saw two small bright lights, up over the crest of the small rise in the woods.

I didn't know there were any house lights over there, I thought, still not getting it. Scanning around the yard with the flashlight again, I returned its light to that area. *There's no house over that way, is there?* Then the "house lights" moved. *What the hell?* Frantically I peered into the deep blackness and made out a head of some type. Coyote? I wasn't sure. Whatever it was, it was watching us. The wind wasn't blowing from that direction so the dogs hadn't been able to scent it. If they had, all hell would have broken loose, because they would have run right over there. And I would have run right after them, trying to save them from getting killed. Totally freaked out, I was somehow able to get the dogs in the house quickly, none the wiser. I was shaking like a leaf by the time I got inside.

The next morning, before I let out the dogs, I walked back to where I'd seen the eyes reflecting. In the fresh snow, I saw the tracks of whatever had been lurking the night before, watching us. The paw prints were *huge*. I held my hand next to one of them and snapped a picture with my phone. My hand is four inches across. These prints were almost that big. Standing up, I followed the trail for a short distance. I have no idea if the prints were from a coyote, or if it was the bobcat. Considering the width of the print, and the claw marks, I'm betting it was the bobcat. Either way, it's not something I want watching me when I'm outside after dark.

The huge paw print compared to my hand

This is my life: stress, mayhem, add a dollop of drama, and you pretty much have my normal day-to-day existence down. If I didn't have to deal with all of it on my own, I wouldn't mind so much, and I would have far fewer grey hairs. Sometimes it feels like me against the world when I walk out my door and have instant PTSD from venturing into the coyote-infested wasteland more commonly known as my backyard. I feel like I always need to watch my back.

When I think about having to daily fight off ferocious predators hell-bent on eating my animals; being outmaneuvered and outflanked by tiny, nefarious, cackling red squirrels; battling continuously for top spot in the herd, and being outsmarted at every turn by my marauding mini horses—I kind of hate to say it, but that condo is looking better and better every day.

And yet, spring comes again, with a promise of life beginning anew. I start to think everything's going to be okay. Until it isn't.

I've been enjoying the view out my dining room window. In the last

24 hours, there have been geese roaming, turkeys parading, mallard ducks swimming in my tiny garden pond, deer noshing on my sumptuously weedy lawn, a hawk perched on a dead oak limb and, the weirdest thing of all, a coyote running full-tilt past my window with a crow flying above it, pecking it repeatedly on the back as it ran. That happened only yesterday afternoon—I'm sure there will be an encore before too long..

The fun never ends.

www.ingramcontent.com/pod-product-compliance
Lightning Source LLC
Chambersburg PA
CBHW070607300426
44113CB00010B/1437